T0167364

What began as a simple desire to help a friend in need has now blossomed into life changing opportunities for over 1400 families in 15 different countries. God has opened up great and effective doors in the fulfillment of His promise that nations would run to us because of the Lord our God (Isaiah 55:5). Surrendering our business to Him was the best decision we ever made, not always the easiest, but definitely the best!

—George & Marla Burns
The Master's Touch | David's 400 Ministries

The Biblical principles that are at the heart and soul of The Master's Touch are clearly taught throughout the Scriptures. Moses taught in Deuteronomy 8:18 that He, alone, gives men and women the ability to accumulate wealth. Joshua states in chapter one verse eight that you must memorize It day and night so that you can carefully obey all that is written in It, then you will prosper and be successful. The Master's Touch sets the example that when we follow God's teaching we shall be successful according to God's promises.

—Dr. Craig Lampe
Pilgrims Walk | The Bible Museum

The Master's Touch and its founders, George and Marla Burns, have become the Biblical blueprint of what I describe as a "Jesus-based" business. Every dynamic of TMT is founded on the Word of God and God truly is first (Matthew 6:33). It has been a God-given honor to oversee and be a part of watching this company and this couple grow in the faith! Praise The Lord.

—Bishop M.L. Moody
Redeemed International Church

THE
BATTLE PLAN:
GOD'S BLUEPRINT
FOR HIS BUSINESS

BRIDGING THE GAP BETWEEN
YOUR PLAN & GOD'S WILL

G & M BURNS

WESTBOW·
PRESS
A DIVISION OF THOMAS NELSON
& ZONDERVAN

God's Holy Word, NKJV, New Sprit Filled Life Bible and the Word Wealth and Kingdom Dynamics contained within It.

Joshua Commentary by James Montgomery Boice

Nehemiah Commentary by James Montgomery Boice

Thru The Bible by James Vernon McGee

Overcoming The Seduction Of Disloyalty by Dr. Jerry Grillo, Jr.

Strong's Exhaustive Concordance Of The Bible

Blueletterbible.org

Dictionary.com

Countless teachings, sermons, and personal discipleship by Bishop M.L.Moody, Redeemed International Church

God's precious Holy Spirit, which leads us into all truth!

WestBow Press books may be ordered through booksellers or by contacting:

WestBow Press
A Division of Thomas Nelson & Zondervan
1663 Liberty Drive
Bloomington, IN 47403
www.westbowpress.com
1 (866) 928-1240

ISBN: 978-1-4908-6224-8 (sc)
ISBN: 978-1-4908-6225-5 (hc)
ISBN: 978-1-4908-6223-1 (e)

Library of Congress Control Number: 2014921595

Printed in the United States of America.

WestBow Press rev. date: 2/3/2014

Contents

To learn more about The Master's Touch
or starting a new business adventure of your own,
visit us at themasterstouch.com
or by phone toll free at 800-868-5406
or in Glendale, Arizona at 623 889-0313.

AUTHOR PREFACE

I remember it very clearly; our journey into entrepreneurship began the first day of January 1996. It was only a couple of days prior that my husband and I were headed home on a road trip from California back to Phoenix, Arizona. In the midst of this long desert drive, George turned and said to me, "I think I want to start a carpet cleaning business." Hmmm, that is interesting I thought... where does he come up with these random ideas? "No, really! Grab a pen. I want you to start writing down some ideas," he told me. "Think about it, every time the guys come to clean our carpets it cost at least $100 and they are in and out in less than an hour. That's a great wage, don't you think?"

You see, George had a background in the military, but was now working in management at a large auto dealership in the Valley. His position and his drive for success had him working from seven A.M. until ten or eleven at night almost every day of the week. Maybe once or at best twice a month, we might have one afternoon together, but that was really about it. I was working in property management at the time for a new construction project in Scottsdale. We made a decent income, but we had no time to do anything together with it. This was one of the most challenging times of our marriage. At this point we had only been married two years, and I had already lost sight of what the point of our marriage was about. We both knew if we didn't make a drastic change things would only continue to get worse. Leaving our supposedly secure income behind to start a carpet cleaning business seemed so crazy at the time, but anything had to be better than the distress, the debt, and the discontentment that we were in!

Okay, so I got my pen out and we started writing down our entire business plan on that life changing ride home. First thing on the to-do list: we traded in my sports car for a used cargo van and some used cleaning equipment. The gentleman who sold us the cleaning equipment was kind enough to take George under his wing and show him the ropes about cleaning carpets and upholstery. So off we went! We both kept our jobs at first while we got the business up and running. By March of the same year I was able to quit my job and put my time and focus into our new endeavor. And, by July, George likewise was out of the car business for good. Praise God!

After a short time in the industry, we began to think about additional services we could expand into. George began to notice how many job sites had natural stone and tile that needed to be cleaned just as much as the carpets. The problem was no tools existed that could effectively restore these surfaces without damaging them.

Remember the man we bought the equipment from? Well, he and George developed a prototype tool that could hook up to the truckmount machine using high pressure and hot water to clean these stone surfaces, making them look like brand new again without damaging the surface. By the end of that year, tile and stone cleaning had become over 80% of our business. Wow, we actually found the niche market. We could perform amazing results for our customers that no one else in the world was doing, how cool is that? Okay, so the world is a big place and we decided we didn't have to be the only kid on the block with this amazing tool. So, we began to manufacture this single-jet tool in our garage and distribute it little by little through the cleaning industry.

Keep in mind, this single-jet wand design only had a four inch head on it. That basically meant you were cleaning the entire floor, one grout line at a time, or roughly 100-200 square feet per hour. It was time for George to put his innovative thinking cap on and design a tool that could cover more square footage in less time. So that is exactly what he did. Although it was three expensive years in the patenting process, a phenomenal tool was turned out. This new design using dual spinning jets was now capable of cleaning 1000-1500 square feet in one hour. That's a ten-fold improvement in design and profitability, and was soon a huge hit in the cleaning industry, locally and nationally.

It was during the time when we were juggling both the cleaning company and the manufacturing company that the Lord really began to tug on our hearts. Again, we had finances and resources to buy all the "toys" we wanted, and we did: house, land, cars, boat, jet skis, ATV's, motorcycles, fifth-wheeler, three horses, and so on and so forth. George had to build a two-story 2400 square foot shop just to store all these so-called toys. But there was still something missing, a void that none of this "stuff" could fulfill. It was a God-shaped void reserved solely for Him! Until we understood that, we were just wasting away all the blessings He was setting before us. What an eye-opener!

Let's fast forward to 2003. We have since sold the cleaning portion of our business and are focused on Turbo Force Manufacturing. We have simplified our lifestyle, and are finally living for Christ first and foremost. A friend of ours approached George and asked if he'd be willing to help him put together the equipment he needed to start up a carpet and tile cleaning company. "Of course!" George responds. After helping our friend get rolling, and seeing his success, we realized what a rush it was to help someone succeed in financial independence. It's life changing!

You see, manufacturing tools for cleaning tile is great, but it is not our passion. However seeing peoples' lives change definitely is! Why not take the experience and knowledge that we have learned over the years and put it into a tangible package that could make a difference in peoples' lives? People like us; stuck in a work environment that they don't know how to get out of; people who have lost their jobs and are not sure what to do; people who just need a chapter change in their life. Let's create a vessel that perhaps God can work through, whether it is for a season or for a lifetime. This is a business opportunity that can change lives. It's called The Master's Touch. We believe and pray that one touch from the Master and they will never be the same again.

God has heard our cry and honored our desires. "Surely you shall call a nation you do not know, and nations who do not know you shall run to you, because of the Lord your God, and the Holy One of Israel; For He has glorified you." (Isaiah 55:5) This is the promise of God that we stand on for our company. He has sent many nations through the doors of our establishment. To Him be all the glory! Our clients don't just learn how to successfully operate a tile cleaning company; they learn how to build their business on Biblical principles. We are not ashamed to share this Truth regardless of where they are from or what they believe. To date (2014), the Lord has enabled us to put into business over 1400 business owners in 15 different countries. God is good!

This David's 400 Battle Plan curriculum is an expansion of what God has already been doing through The Master's Touch. It is our prayer that regardless of what business endeavor you choose to embark in, that you would do it according to God's will and God's ways for yourself, your family, and certainly for Him.

In His service,
George & Marla Burns

INTRODUCTION

CHAPTER ONE:
Welcome To Biblical Entrepreneurship

Welcome to David's 400 Battle Plan and Biblical Entrepreneurship. You now hold the tools to help you navigate the crossroads of your life and your new business. You are about to embark on a learning experience that may very well oppose everything you have already learned according to the world's perspective for a successful business. "For My thoughts are not your thoughts, nor are your ways My ways, says the Lord. For as the heavens are higher than the earth, so are My ways higher than your ways and My thoughts than your thoughts." (Isaiah 55:8-9)

What Does This Mean To You And Me?
There is a way that seems right to a man (Proverbs 14:12). But, the Lord who sits in the heavens laughs at man's plans (Psalm 2:4). How much better would it be if our so-called plans aligned with God's perfect will for our lives? David's 400 Battle Plan is about bridging these two chasms together.

Before King David officially took the throne, he had many lessons to learn about running a kingdom according to God's plan. King Saul, David's predecessor, may have been the people's choice, but the Scriptures tell us that David was God's choice, for he was a man after God's own heart (Acts 13:22).

When David was on the run from King Saul, he took refuge in a cave called Adullam. It was there that, "everyone who was in distress, everyone who was in debt, and everyone who was discontented gathered to him. So he became captain over them and there were about 400 men with him." (1 Samuel 22:2) Under King David's leadership, this ragtag group of men accomplished many great exploits for the kingdom of God. Wouldn't you like to tap into some of their strategic plans for yourself and your business? Well, you can... It's time for God's battle plan and the model of David's 400.

David's 400 Battle Plan is an interactive program designed to help you build, maintain and further your business based on five pillars fundamental to building a successful faith-based company. Within this teaching you will find many effective tools and techniques that will provide core principles for both the business arena and your personal life. It is our ambition to clearly and effectively teach these Biblical revelations in a way that will influence how you run your business. We're confident that when such truths are laid out, it will make a huge impact on the foundation and the future of your business.

Biblical Entrepreneurship
There are many rewards to starting your own business. To be successful you must be prepared, count the costs and move forward in faith regardless of the field you choose.

"For which of you, intending to build a tower, does not sit down first and count the cost, whether he has enough to finish it..." -Luke 14:28-32

Entrepreneurship Defined
What does it mean to be an entrepreneur? Merriam-Webster defines entrepreneurship as "one who initiates a business and is willing to risk loss in order to make money." Dictionary.com defines entrepreneur as "a person who organizes and manages any enterprise, especially a business." We define it as "the willingness to take the initiative plus the necessary risks involved to start, organize, and manage a business based on faith."

What Makes Entrepreneurs Successful?
The definition of success is different for all of us. For some, success is defined by money, cars, houses or lots of toys. Others define it by their accomplishments or by the number of relationships forged. Maybe you define it by newfound freedom of time, or perhaps by your ability to give back to others or your community. Regardless of how you define success, all genuine entrepreneurs possess the following traits.

Commitment

Entrepreneurs will make a commitment to the success of their business. They will carry the desire to take on responsibilities and see that tasks are completed. They will overcome objections and find the appropriate means to complete the task at hand. True entrepreneurs are willing to commit their time, talent, treasure, temple and thoughts into what they believe to be a successful opportunity.

Leadership

Leaders have the ability to inspire and encourage others to reach the objectives set forth in front of them. They are good communicators and good delegators. They are willing to make decisions and accept the consequences. In order to successfully lead, leaders must first be able to follow; and in order to be of authority, they must also be under authority. A good leader leads by example.

Faith

Faith is the key to the success of every entrepreneur. Starting any new endeavor requires faith. Faith is an action based on a belief sustained by sure confidence. Faith is the confident belief in what you are about to embark on before you see the manifestation of that thing or that endeavor come to pass. Without faith, it is impossible to succeed in any forward motion and without faith it is impossible to please God (Hebrews 11:6). Faith is more than just believing; it is acting on that belief... action that is motivated by the confidence that God has placed in you by His Word. Try remembering it by this simple acronym. ABC: Action + Belief + Confidence = Faith!

Battle Plan Blueprint

God's Word is packed full of plans and prints for conducting battle, not just literally on a battlefield, but for the spiritual battles that all believers face otherwise known as warfare. What soldier goes into battle without being properly equipped? Perhaps only the foolish one!

When you lift up the name of Jesus in the day-to-day operations of your faith-based company, there will be battles. At times, it may seem like all-out war. But even in this, fear not, for during such trials your faith is being made strong! After all, if you were not bold for Christ, you would not be a threat to Satan or his demonic forces.

In the apostle Paul's letter to the Ephesians, he writes about getting battle ready... How? By putting on the "full armor of God" (Ephesians 6:10-18).

We do this so that we may be able to not only stand, but fight against the wiles of the Devil; for we do not wrestle against flesh and blood, but against principalities and powers. Friends, this means the battle is in the mind.

Your best defense is to "Put on the mind of Christ" (Philippians 2:5). To the Corinthian church, Paul admonishes that we must, "Bring every thought into captivity to the obedience of Christ" (2 Corinthians 10:5b). This can only be done by staying renewed in God's Word on a daily basis. It is His Word that brings us into obedience, delivers us from evil, and declares victories over our enemies. God's Word has much to say pertaining to battles. Here are just a few of our favorite verses on the subject...

"Then all this assembly shall know that the Lord does not save with sword and spear; for the battle is the Lord's, and He will give you into our hands." -1 Samuel 17:47 (David defeats Goliath)

"I have pursued my enemies and destroyed them; neither did I turn back again till they were destroyed. And I have destroyed them and wounded them, so that they could not rise; they have fallen under my feet. For You have armed me with strength for the battle; You have subdued under me those who rose against me." -2 Samuel 22:38-40 (David's deliverance)

"And it shall be, when you hear a sound of marching in the tops of the mulberry trees, then you shall go out to battle, for God has gone out before you to strike the camp of the Philistines. So David did as God commanded him, and they drove back the army of the Philistines." -1 Chronicles 14:15-16 (David established as king over Jerusalem)

"You will not need to fight in this battle. Position yourselves, stand still and see the salvation of the Lord, who is with you, O Judah and Jerusalem! Do not fear or be dismayed; tomorrow go out against them, for the Lord is with you." - 2 Chronicles 20:17 (King Jehoshaphat's deliverance)

The Starting Position
This course assumes the position that you have already gone through the legal ramifications of starting a new business. We strongly encourage you to consult with your accountant when working through the important legal details.

The "Battle Plan" herein for the faith-based company will begin by focusing on choosing a proper business name with a recognizable brand icon, selecting a banner Scripture and writing a vision statement. Even if your business is already operational, taking the time to make sure you have these basic foundations accurately in place will be an asset to you and your business.

CHAPTER TWO:
Names With Meanings
& Branding Icons

Choosing Your Business Name

Your business name is very important; it's the first contact that a prospective client will have with you and your business. Choose a power-packed name that is catchy, memorable, and says what you do.

What Is In A Name?

To find that answer, let's take a closer look at the Hebrew and Greek root meanings of the word "name." In the Old Testament, it is referred to as "shem" meaning fame, memorial, character. In the New Testament, it is referred to as "onama" meaning identity of intrinsic value and its abilities. So then a name is not just a name, but rather it represents its owner's character, abilities, identity and for what it or they are to be remembered.

God speaks volumes in and through names. When we pray in the name of Jesus, we pray in the power of attorney and full backing of what that name represents. Look at the examples found in the names of Jabez (O.T.) and Jason (N.T.). Both are obscure passages, hard to find, and even a bit peculiar, yet packed full of powerful meaning, rich character and helpful insight. You might consider avoiding names such as Judas, Jezebel or Jehoiakim. Remember the intrinsic value of something is found within its name, so choose wisely; your business name will represent your company's full onama character.

You can find out more about Jabez in 1 Chronicles 4:9-10. And see for yourself what Jason represents in Acts 17:1-14.

Brainstorm & Feedback

If you haven't settled on a name for your business yet, take time to brainstorm some ideas. Attempt to come up with something that is both catchy and memorable. Most importantly, does it represent you, your business and what you do? Make a list of some potential names for your business and then see what kind of feedback you get from friends and family. Be sure to ask those who will be honest with you and not just flatter you. This is no time to engage with the spirit of divination. Be sure to do a Google search to see if that name or a similar name has already been exhausted in your area or in your industry.

Tally up the responses to your potential name choices and see what favorites land at the top of the list. However, we do not want you to stop here. There is more to consider than just man's opinion on this subject. [Note: A neutral response is basically the same as a negative response.]

Some advisors have influenced companies to choose a name that begins with a letter that appears early in the alphabet for the preliminary benefit of an early listing in the phone directory and other alphabetized listings. Although there is some truth to this, our advice is to choose a solid name with a powerful meaning and let God sort it out. In other words, trust God, confirm the name in His Word, and move forward in faith. Here are some ideas to further assist you in coming up with a name that will represent you and your business.

Start by choosing a key word that describes or incorporates one main element of what your business will offer. For example, if you were going to start a pest control business, a few key words might be: pest, annoying, elimination, drive out, or exit. Next, if you intend for your business name to carry the weight of a Biblical backing, you'll need to look up these key words in a concordance. You can use the one in the back of your Bible, though it is often limited, or you might try the free online resource from blueletterbible.org. It will contain a greater amount of detail and is more efficient in finding what you need quickly.

As you look up each of your key words, take note of the context for which they appear in the Scriptures. When used in its proper context, does it correlate to what your business represents? Does it catch your attention in a personal way? Let's go back to our pest control example. The key words "drive out" leads us to a passage in Exodus 23:30, "Little by little I will drive them out from before you, until you have increased, and you inherit the land."

This verse, of course, is referring to driving out people, but not just any people. It refers to driving out the enemy from before Israel. Most homeowners will easily agree that unwanted pests in their home is enemy number one. Another type and shadow in this verse is how Christ, as the Angel of the Lord, will drive out our enemies, those annoying things that come to steal our joy and rob us of our peace. The power of Jesus' name destroys the authority of the one who binds us to chaos, the chaos of the world, of our own flesh and of the devil. He drives them out that we might be brought in. This verse successfully relates to the core value and nature of this business example. With that said, what better name than, "Exodus Pest Control - We Drive Them out!"

Creating A Logo Or Brand Icon
The second thing that will catch the attention of your potential client is the logo or brand icon that you choose. You may be thinking, "What is the difference?" Well, in our case it was a $9,400.00 difference, but we'll discuss that later. Interestingly enough, both logo and icon come from Biblical roots.

Logo: a symbol or small design adopted by an organization to identify its products or services. It originated from the Greek word logos, which means word or indescribable thing. Hmmm interesting... logos is then a symbol that is considered indescribable yet identifiable. It is interesting that the apostle John chose this word to describe Christ in the opening paragraph of his gospel account.

"In the beginning was the Word (Logos), and the Word (Logos) was with God, and the Word (Logos) was God. He was in the beginning with God. All things were made through Him, and without Him nothing was made that was made. In Him was life, and the life was the light of men." -John 1:1-4

The Power Of A Well-Branded Icon
Let's consider one of the most well known logo-icons that exist on this earth, the cross. Regardless of what color, material, or finish it comes in, all will recognize it as a cross. Many may not know the full message and power that is associated with this symbol, but nonetheless, they will still characterize this icon in some way with our Lord Jesus Christ. The apostle Paul writes in his letter to Corinth, "For the message of the cross is foolishness to those who are perishing, but to us who are being saved it

is the power of God." Whether we are foolish or wise, the cross will always be a recognized symbol of what Christ did upon it some 2000 years ago. Now, that's a powerful logo! So, to the wise, if you can choose a logo or icon that carries that much weight, you'll be in business!

Logo or Icon?

As previously mentioned, the difference for us between a logo and an icon was $9,400.00. Our first experience with professional logo artists landed our company with a very attractive logo for about $600.00. We were able to get a clean, simple, and well-recognizable logo that we otherwise were not able to create on our own, or with the programs that we had available to us at the time. This logo served us well for some time.

Now, many years later, as our business expanded and became more diversified, it was time for a new name and a new look. This time our team traveled out of state to meet with a brand icon specialist. This process consisted of three nine-hour days in a closed room of intense brainstorming. The most important elements from that adventure are included in this chapter. One thing the specialist stressed when creating an icon image, is that you should like it first when it is rendered in a black and white image. Secondly, it should be clearly visible when displayed at the size of a U.S. Quarter. Their motto was, "If you don't like it when it's small and monochromatic, then making it bigger and multi-colored only makes it bigger and more colorful, but not better!" This advice came at the tune of $10,000.00.

We started with some hand drawn conceptual images within a 2" square. Just like your business name, your icon also needs to clearly represent who you are and what you are doing. As a representation of you and your business, your icon design should be able to stand alone without any text. Below is the registered trademark and brand icon for "The Master's Touch."

This brand icon clearly illustrates a cross as well as a crossroad. It also represents a narrow road and a wide road. It indicates that in the course of life, you may encounter a crossroad of choices, a place where you may need to alter your direction, a place where you were traveling on one path, but God has placed another path before you, a place where one touch from the Master may change your life.

CHAPTER THREE:
Banner Scripture & Vision Statement

Choosing A Banner Scripture

If God has given you a clear vision for your business, then He's surely given you a promise to go with it, and confirmed that promise by His Word. His Word is filled with over 8,800 promises, all of which you can say, "yes and amen" in Him. In other words, you can come into full agreement with each of these promises over your personal life as well as the life of your business. You can stand on these promises knowing that His Word is forever settled in heaven, and that what He has said and declared He will surely do according to His perfect will.

A banner Scripture is a Scripture that you stand on as an individual and will stand on as a company. It's personal, it's public, and it lets people know where you stand. In times of trials, holding firm to the promises of God, and reminding Him of the promises that He has so graciously given you, will be a backbone to your faith-based company!

Just like choosing a name, it is the same application for locating a banner Scripture for your business. Start by looking up the key words that represent the core values you stand on as a company in your Bible's concordance, or use the online resources of blueletterbible.org. Remember the example for Exodus Pest Control, the banner Scripture for this company would be Exodus 23:30. When searching for a banner Scripture, it's likely the Holy Spirit will lead you through verses that are relative to what God has done and is doing in your life now, as well as what He will do through your business.

Many first time business owners struggle greatly with the warfare that exists between faith and fear. There are many rewards to starting your own business, but if you can't overcome the obstacle of fear, you will never experience them for yourself. Being an entrepreneur is a huge faith step! Knowing that fear is not from God, yet it continues to plague so many, The Master's Touch stands on the Scriptures that reinforce the promises of God concerning fear.

"For God has not given us a spirit of fear, but of power and of love and of a sound mind." -2 Timothy 1:7

Your Banner Scripture
Use your banner Scripture both on marketing materials and in your workplace. If you are building your business on the solid foundation of Christ Jesus, then we encourage you not to be ashamed to let people know that you are a faith-based company. Be bold, stand firm and lean on Him!

Writing A Vision Statement
A vision statement is a vivid description written and inspired by successful leaders to clearly and concisely convey the direction, purpose and values of the organization. It is a written mental image of how you see your business both now and in the future.

A powerful vision statement should stretch expectations and aspirations, helping you to step out of your comfort zone and into a faith zone. By compiling a clear vision statement, you can effectively communicate your intentions and motivate your team to look ahead to the common vision of your organization. Your vision statement should create a mental picture that inspires, energizes, and opens the eyes of those who read it and what is possible to those who believe. When you believe all things are possible according to God's will for your life and your business, you begin to realize that dreams can be achieved, that challenges can be conquered, and that problems can be solved. In doing so you open up a completely new set of avenues and possibilities.

Albert Einstein said, "Imagination is more powerful than knowledge." In respect to this, knowledge allows you to see things as they are, but imagination, like faith, allows you to see things as they could be. Describe your vision statement in the present tense, as well as the future tense. Add sensory details that build a clear image of your ideal outcome. Include the Biblical principles that motivate you and your business.

Incorporate your banner Scripture as part of your statement. Let those who read your statement share in the vision that God has given you and stand confident on His promise that He who has begun a good work in you will complete it. (Philippians 1:6)

"I will stand my watch and set myself on the rampart, and watch to see what He will say to me, and what I will answer when I am corrected. Then the Lord answered me and said: 'Write the vision and make it plain on tablets, that he may run who reads it. For the vision is yet for an appointed time; but at the end it will speak, and it will not lie. Though it tarries, wait for it; because it will surely come, it will not tarry. Behold the proud, his soul is not upright in him; but the just shall live by his faith.' " -Habakkuk 2:1-4

Sample Vision Statement
The Master's Touch Fitness Centers - A complete wellness center that caters to the Christian lifestyle, including constantly varied movements in group and individual fitness, mobility and recovery, nutrition programs, chiropractic care, massage therapy, and much more; an atmosphere filled with praise and worship music that encourages and motivates; a place to be transformed by the renewing of the mind and discipline of the body; a place where those who are physically fit, yet spiritually dead, can be transformed from the inside out. Core values and core training are fundamental along with challenging activities and accountability generated through healthy competitive group fitness.

PILLAR 1: BUILDING RELATIONSHIPS

CHAPTER FOUR: Relationship Objectives & Principles

Biblical Relationships

They begin with the acknowledgment that your own will, wants, and selfish desires must take a backseat to God's will, design, and call on your life and on your business. One of the key elements required in all relationships is trust. The Lord is seeking those who will trust and obey Him, and through such actions, a loving and trusting relationship develops. Follow God's example as you build your business with integrity that your clients can trust in. Along with trust must come humbleness. Let your clients see that they matter more to you than you matter to yourself. It's no secret that customers want to feel like they are more than just a number or dollar sign.

There are many ways business owners can build strong relationships with their clients. Some of these ways include: knowing your client's name, acknowledging the value of their repeat business, accommodating their special needs, consistently delivering service with honesty and superiority, and most of all, communicating regularly with your clients. All of these topics and more will be covered in this chapter.

"He has shown you, O man, what is good; and what does the Lord require of you but to do justly, to love mercy, and to walk humbly with your God?"
- Micah 6:8

What Is A Relationship?

Concerning business, it is defined as the way in which two or more people or organizations regard and behave toward one another. How you regard or how you behave toward someone can make a huge difference in any given relationship.

If you regard someone with respect and honesty, you're likely to be given trust in return. This is seen in the simple factor of reciprocity. Reciprocity speaks of mutual actions by different parties or elements that work together to produce the same result. In other words, if you want loyalty from your clients, then give them loyalty. If you want repeat business from your clients, then give them consistency. On the flip side, if you're only concerned with the one-time sale, then treat them like they are just another number.

A unifying relationship consists of two or more people who have at least one similarity of interest or characteristic. The common denominator between the business owner and his client is that one has something that the other wants.

How you regard and behave toward one another in the exchanging relationship is a key element to your success. Indeed, the old saying of "what goes around comes around" can certainly be applied here. As we continue to unfold what relationships are, why we have them, and how to effectively build and maintain them, we'll be using many familiar and some not so familiar relationships revealed in the Holy Scriptures in a variety of thought provoking ways for many of our key examples.

What Is The Objective Of Relationships?

To some the answer may be fellowship, companionship, or entertainment; to others it may be resources or profitability. Understanding the objective of a relationship is pivotal to even having a relationship in the first place.

For example, to understand God the Father, we must understand Jesus Christ His Son; and in order to understand Jesus, we must understand His Holy Spirit. Starting with the Holy Spirit, what is the objective of His relationship to you? Answer: The key objective of the Holy Spirit is to guide men into all truth by pointing them to Jesus, to His life, His death and His resurrection (John 14:26, 15:26, 16:13-14). No man can come to Christ unless he has been drawn by the power of the Holy Spirit (John 15:16).

This brings us to the objective relationship of Christ. Jesus said in John 14:6. "I am the way, the truth, and the life. No one comes to the Father except through Me." The key objective of Christ's relationship with those who believe is that of the mediator between man and God and as the propitiation for our sins (1 John 4:9-10).

And lastly, the key objective of your relationship with God the Father is reconciliation, which is achieved in only one way, through a relationship with Christ, His Son, as drawn by the Holy Spirit. Each of these relationships has a specific objective that must be understood in order to move forward in that relationship.

You can read more about the Trinity relationship in Matthew 3:16-17, 28:19; John 1:1-2, 10:30, 17:11+21; Acts 2:32-33; and 2 Corinthians 13:14, just to name a few.

The Objective Of Your Business Relationships
Now that we've covered the ultimate objective relationship of the Godhead Trinity, it's time to think about what your objectives are in building a relationship with your clients.

Unifying relationships require a common interest. Is the common interest between you and your client simply just your product or service, or is there something greater? Just as the flesh-man is attracted to the things of the world, so likewise the spirit-man is attracted to the things of the spirit. It won't take long for a faith-based company to see the reciprocity of a spirit-filled place of business naturally attracting the spirit-filled believer through it's doors or website.

What does your business have in common with your prospective clients? What is the main objective that you want to establish between your business and your clients? Are you looking for a one-time sale or repeat business? Are you seeking loyalty from your clients? Do you care if they shop the competition? Are you looking for referrals from your clients? Understand what your key relationship objective is with your clients. It will aid you in keeping your focus in the correct perspective.

What Does The Lord Require In His Relationship?
Beginning in the Pentateuch, Moses gave Israel 613 commandments pertaining to their relationship with the Lord and with one another. David reduced these down to eleven commandments in Psalm 15:1-5. Isaiah

later reduced them to six in Isaiah 33:15, then Micah reduced them to three in Micah 6:8. Isaiah further reduces them down to two in Isaiah 56:1-2, then Habakkuk narrows it down to one commandment; "The just shall live by faith."

The Greatest Commandment

The principle that the Lord is seeking in a relationship with Him is the same principle that you are to exchange between relationships with one another. The apostle John quotes Jesus best in his gospel message...

"A new commandment I give to you, that you love one another; as I have loved you, that you also love one another. By this all will know that you are My disciples, if you have love for one another." -John 13:34-35

"This is My commandment, that you love one another as I have loved you. Greater love has no one than this, than to lay down one's life for his friends. You are My friends if you do whatever I command you. No longer do I call you servants, for a servant does not know what his master is doing; but I have called you friends, for all things that I heard from My Father I have made known to you. You did not choose Me, but I chose you and appointed you that you should go and bear fruit, and that your fruit should remain, that whatever you ask the Father in My name He may give you. These things I command you, that you love one another." -John 15:12-17

To walk humbly before God, and to love the Lord and to love one another are basic principles of the life of faith. The actions resulting from such love are based on the faith of Christ working through you and in your business.

So what is really meant by "love one another?" Let's take a look at how the apostle Paul describes love. Speaking of himself he tells the believers in Corinth that if he has faith that can move mountains, but has not love, he is nothing; or if he gave everything he owned to feed the poor, but has not love, it profits him nothing. He goes on to say...

"Love suffers long and is kind; love does not envy; love does not parade itself, is not puffed up; does not behave rudely, does not seek its own, is not provoked, thinks no evil; does not rejoice in iniquity, but rejoices in the truth; bears all things, believes all things, hopes all things, endures all things. Love never fails. But whether there are prophecies, they will fail; whether there are tongues, they will cease; whether there is knowledge, it will vanish away... And now abide faith, hope, love, these three; but the greatest of these is love." -1 Corinthians 13:4-8 & 13

Loving In Today's Business Arena

By now, you may be asking, "Is that even possible?" Could Paul's message remotely still apply to today's businessperson? Well, the Hebrew writer tells us that God is the same yesterday, today and forever. King David, the prophet Isaiah, and the disciples, Matthew and Peter, all transcribed that the Word of the Lord endures forever. This brings us to an important and pivotal point; if you intend to build your business on Biblical principles, you must settle in your heart, that every Word of God is pure and that He is a shield to those who put their trust in Him (Proverbs 30:5-6). Faithing and trusting in God's Word means to literally hang your body on His promises without losing hope.

About this "love thing," how do you go about loving someone that you're not even sure you like? Breaking down Paul's exhortation on love will provide an array of valuable insights to the application of love in the business arena. God told Moses little by little you shall inherit the land, and He likewise told Isaiah that He would teach knowledge and give understanding to those who would listen and heed the message line upon line and precept upon precept. With that said, it's time to sit down, buckle up, and put your thinking cap on.

It Is Patient: Parenting isn't the only thing that requires patience. Staff and clients alike will admire one who is patient, especially when your patience is being tried at all levels. Patience requires waiting on the Lord in your decisions and yes, "It is still a virtue."

It Is Kind: Kindness is shown through your actions as well as your attitude. It is the visible attribute of an invisible heart posture. It is among the fruits distributed by the Spirit (Galatians 5:22). It can be as simple as greeting every individual with a smile and warm welcome the moment they walk in the door, leaving no one unnoticed.

It Is Not Envious: Jealousy is a deal breaker in any relationship. It drove King Saul to utter madness, leaving him with a spirit of distress, a life of paranoia and disobedient actions. It ultimately cost him the kingdom.

Your business is a type of kingdom, which God has given you to reign over and oversee. When left unchecked, envy is a sure fire way to its destruction.

It Does Not Brag: Boasters are third on the list that Paul rebukes in his letter to Timothy (2 Timothy 3:1-5). King Hezekiah, even after all the good he had done, fell short in this area when he unwisely showed the men of Babylon all the treasures of his house. Babylon was an enemy he was at peace with, but nonetheless, his boasting created vulnerability to the entire kingdom. Beware of boasting to your staff or to your friendly competition. Loose lips sink ships!

It Is Not Puffed Up: Pride is number four on Paul's list and it always comes before the fall! The spirit of pride loves to take all the credit for itself and is usually accompanied by presumption. King Azariah was prosperous and resourceful, but his pride and presumption of stepping out of his office (king) and into another (priest) got him stricken with leprosy and led to a life of isolation.

It Is Not Rude: Rude behavior is that which is unbecoming or inappropriate and lacking subtlety, often considered as ignorant and uneducated. What is classified as rude is a relative term to each person individually. To some smoking is rude, to others it is not. Both John and Paul write about living and acting according to your own convictions. As you are transformed by the renewing of our mind through God's Word, your convictions continually grow closer to His will and His ways for your life and your business. There are things you may have gotten away with as a child, but no longer entertain as an adult. Many experienced businessmen conduct their business differently now than when they first began. Let your conscience move you from an uneducated rudeness to knowledgeable revelations in your life and in your business.

It Is Not Self-Serving: Others know when your motives are only to seek your own desires. Letting others know they matter more to you than you matter to yourself is not only worthwhile, but also essential. Jonathan, son of King Saul, displayed this in his relationship with David.

It Is Not Easily Angered: When provoked, you have the option to either react or respond. Reactions are committed in haste and often done out of anger or retaliation. Those who respond with deliberation take time to assess the situation before allowing anger to take hold.

It Is Not Resentful: Bitterness and unforgiveness are the evil roots of resentment. It is a continual state of anguish of the soul and is spiritual poison affecting all who come in contact with it. Forgiveness is the key to breaking the bonds of resentment. No business can survive if a root of bitterness remains (Hebrews 12:14-15). Chop it down quickly that a tender shoot of believing, faithing, praising, thanking and giving can grow in it's place.

It Is Not Glad About Injustice: Injustice, like iniquity, is defined as unrighteousness of heart and is often considered an act of unfairness. King David understood this ideal; for despite all the harm King Saul meant toward David, he would not rejoice over his demise or his death.

It Rejoices In The Truth: Whom the Son has set free is free indeed, what better reason is there to celebrate? In like manner, let there be no division in your business. If one member suffers, all the members suffer; and if one is honored, let all the members rejoice with him (1 Cor 12:26).

It Bears All Things: Believers are called to bear one another's burdens and so fulfill the law of Christ. For if anyone thinks himself to be something, when he is nothing, he deceives himself (Galatians 6:2-3). In other words, humble yourself and be willing to help others in need.

It Believes All Things: This is not gullible naiveness, but rather an intellectual faith that holds confidence in what has been proven credible. It is the ability to trust without doubting. If you lack wisdom in the area in which you are to believe, ask God, who gives to all liberally and without reproach, and it will be given to you. But you must ask in faith, without doubting, for he who doubts is a double-minded man, unstable in all his ways (James 1:5-8).

It Hopes In All Things: This hope involves trust and requires waiting in joy with confidence. When you have sown seed in good ground in the midst of your business, do not grow weary in doing good, for in due season you shall reap if you do not lose heart (Galatians 6:9).

It Endures All Things: Endurance in the Greek is "hupomeno;" meaning to hold one's ground in conflict, to bear up against adversity, hold out under stress, stand firm, persevere under pressure, wait calmly and courageously. It is not mere patience, but the active, energetic resistance to defeat that allows calm and brave endurance. All entrepreneurs need hupomeno endurance!

It Never Ends: Failing involves quitting, which is not the kind of love described here. Agape love is unconditional, undefeatable and without end. It is self-giving without asking anything in return. Agape is more a love by choice than a love by chance, and it refers to the will rather than the emotion. Agape describes the unconditional love God has for His children.

It Is To Be Given To Others Just As God Has Given It To You: Just as Christ freely gave everything on your account when you were still a sinner and afar off from Him, likewise you are called to give in the same manner. Giving is to be done with a pure heart and not out of guilt or selfish ambition. It is the proof text of the Spirit in you. When Matthew quotes Jesus saying, "I desire mercy and not sacrifice," it is a reflection of the heart posture of the one giving. Your heart posture is everything. God values your relationship with Him more than He desires your service for Him. Paul writes to Timothy, "The purpose of the commandment is love from a pure heart, from a good conscience, and from sincere, unhypocritical faith." Freely give to your staff and to your clients out of what the Lord has so graciously given you.

It Makes Sacrifices For Others: Matthew, Mark, and Luke all speak of how the first shall be last and the last shall be first; and he who exalts himself will be humbled, and he who humbles himself will be exalted, for God resists the proud but gives grace to the humble. True humility puts the concerns of others before oneself. Humility involves submission, and submission requires setting your wants and desires aside and coming under the authority of another. Are you willing to submit to another's authority? If not, don't expect others to submit to you.

It Bears Fruit That Remains: What is the fruit that should grow in your business? The apostle Paul describes this as the fruit of the spirit: love, joy, peace, patience, kindness, goodness, faithfulness, gentleness and self-control. Luke quotes Jesus saying, "A good man out of the good treasure of his heart brings forth good; and an evil man out of the evil treasure of his heart brings forth evil. For out of the abundance of the heart his mouth speaks." Therefore, bear good fruit not only in your own life, but throughout your company as well. As you abide in Him, these will abide in you. Love is the evidence that you are His disciple!

We have uncovered some of the elements of love in the business arena, but what about the other requirements mentioned in the opening verse of this chapter...

"He has shown you, O man, what is good; and what does the Lord require of you but to do justly, to love mercy, and to walk humbly with your God?" - Micah 6:8

Notice the parts of speech used in this earmark verse... verbs require an action! To do, to love, and to walk all require movement, not just any movement, but a forward motion. Without movement of some kind, it is very easy for relationships to become stagnant and unproductive.

A stagnant business relationship is very similar to a stagnate pool of water. When water ceases to run or flow it becomes stale or foul. It creates a harmful environment and development, growth, and life all begin to fail. The same things occur when communication is stopped up in a relationship. Without consistent contact with your clients, development and growth begin to cease.

CHAPTER FIVE:
The Building Process

Building your business and your business relationships on a solid foundation is a must. In this way, building a business is much like building a house. If a house is not built on solid ground and if the footer is not dug deep enough, over time, the home runs the risk of shifting or failing. Some things to consider; all buildings are required to have blueprints before construction can begin. Once underway, a well-built house must have a chief cornerstone, quality materials, and a reliable overhead covering. Throughout this chapter pertaining to Pillar 1: Building Relationships we will expand on this building process and how it relates to your business.

"Therefore whoever hears these sayings of Mine, and does them, I will liken him to a wise man who built his house on the rock: and the rain descended, the floods came, and the winds blew and beat on that house; and it did not fall, for it was founded on the rock. But everyone who hears these sayings of Mine, and does not do them, will be like a foolish man who built his house on the sand: and the rain descended, the floods came, and the winds blew and beat on that house; and it fell. And great was its fall. And so it was, when Jesus had ended these sayings, that the people were astonished at His teaching, for He taught them as one having authority, and not as the scribes." -Matthew 7:24-29

Before you can even begin to lay a foundation, you must first count the cost of what you are about to embark in. Let's look at Luke's quote in chapter 14:28-30 referring to the cost of discipleship: "For which of you, intending to build a tower, (or in this case business) does not sit down first and count the cost, whether he has enough to finish it - lest, after he has laid the foundation, and is not able to finish, all who see it begin to mock him, saying 'This man began to build and was not able to finish.' "

Have You Counted The Cost?

Do not be surprised when men revile and persecute you, and say all kinds of evil against you falsely for Christ's sake. Instead of shrinking back in fear or despair, rejoice and be exceedingly glad, for great is your reward in heaven, for so they persecuted the prophets who were before you (Matthew 5:12).

Even after you have counted the cost, there will still be mockers. King David cried out in the psalms many times regarding those who hated him without a cause, and how they have increased who troubled him, for many were they who rose up against him, saying there is no help for him in God. But the good news is the Lord is a shield for you, He is your glory, and the One who lifts your head. Fear not, for He hears your cry and He shall sustain you! (Psalm 3)

Christ forewarned us in the book of Matthew, they hated Him and His Father who sent Him before they ever hated you. Now, after receiving all that, are you still ready to build your business on Biblical principles? It's important to make your call and election sure. Let these truths not bring fear of persecution, but confidence in the promise. He who builds his house or business upon the Rock shall surely stand, for all other is sinking sand. So, now that you've counted the cost and made your election sure, it's time to move forward in faith.

Choosing Good Ground

The first thing to determine when building a foundation is its location. What is the condition of the ground you are about to build on? Is it solid or is it unstable? In the parable of the wise and foolish builders (Matthew 7:24-29 & Luke 6:46-49), Jesus is comparing these builders to those who hear His teachings and do them and those who hear but do not do them.

To build on solid ground means to build on and with those who not only listen but also heed the teachings in God's Word. James, the brother of our Lord, puts it this way....

"But be doers of the Word, and not hearers only, deceiving yourselves. For if anyone is a hearer of the Word and not a doer, he is like a man observing his natural face in a mirror; for he observes himself, goes away, and immediately forgets what kind of man he was. But he who looks into the perfect law of liberty and continues his attention there, and does not become a forgetful hearer but a doer of the work, he will be blessed in what he does." -James 1:22-25

Have you ever known someone who comes to you for advice, but no matter what you say, they continue in their own agenda anyway? It leaves you wondering why did they come to you in the first place. This is the exact type of character that Matthew and Luke call foolish. They hear you and appear to be listening, but on the contrary, they do not do as you advise. This is the unstable ground that you do not want to build on, not with your staff, and not with your clients! For when the first strong winds of adversity come, they are carried away, for they have not built any solid foundation on which to stand. Their folly lies with the fact that they have heard what is right, have acknowledged that it is right and profess to be following it, but yet they still do not put Christ's teachings into practice. Speaking of the one who hears and does, Christ says, "But he who received seed on the good ground is he who hears the word and understands it, who indeed bears fruit and produces: some a hundredfold, some sixty, some thirty." (Matthew 13:23) It is vital that the ground you build your relationships on is good ground. From good ground will spring forth good fruit, and good fruit is good for a good business.

A Solid Foundation
The foundation of your house is one of the most important tasks when building your home. If the foundation is not properly laid then the entire edifice will be unstable. The same truth applies to building your business and the relationships surrounding your business. Let's begin by looking at the two comparatively.

Some of the basic steps in preparing a natural foundation consist of surveying the land, excavating the surface soil, preparing footers and temporary forms, running electrical lines and plumbing systems, and securing anchoring beams. Comparatively the steps for the foundation of your business relationships might consist of the following...

First, understand what boundaries God has revealed to you concerning your business. Survey and stake out relationships that compliment the footprints in God's Word (Proverbs 2:20). Relationships formed outside Biblical perimeters will surely lead to disasters. Excavation of our fleshly "topsoil" is also an important step. Rid your business of mere outward appearances and operate with a pure heart of genuine integrity.

Temporary forms - keep newly formed relationships close to you until they become strengthened and mature enough to handle situations on their own (Ruth and Naomi are a great example of this). Concerning the power supply, to have power you must be connected to the source of that power. God's Word is the power supply delivered through His Holy Spirit to His saints. Staying connected to Him is the lifeline in any sustaining relationship.

A good plumbing system is like having trustworthy relationships that keep things flowing accordingly. They are great at watching for signs of backup or potential damage (i.e. gossip, mocking, complaining, etc.).

Anchor Beams - prepare your foundation with a solid anchor in Christ's teachings and Paul's writings. You, yourself, must be bolted down in order to support the framework of others. As you are anchored, you'll be able to receive others with joy and gladness. (Hebrews 6:19-20)

You Must Have Both: Good Ground And A Solid Foundation
You can't have a solid foundation without building on good ground; and you can't build on good ground without a solid foundation. The same applies to the parable of the wise and foolish builders. You cannot have the teachings of Christ without Christ; and you cannot have Christ without Christ's teachings. In other words you can't have Him without His ethics and you can't have His ethics without Him. Remember, the greatest ethic of all is to simply live by His faith! A solid foundation that is built on good ground allows you to be at peace in times of trouble, knowing that your business will surely stand firm.

Bottom line: We must build on both. One: Build your business relationships with those who hear, heed and follow your advice and your authority as it aligns with God's Word. Two: Build your business relationships on the solid foundation of Jesus Christ. He is the footing, the forms, the anchor and the One who carries the load of the burden. So, cast your load and your burden on Him, for it matters to Him about you. (1 Peter 5:7)

Chief Cornerstone
Every well-built building begins with a cornerstone. It is the first stone that you lay and it is the starting block to which all other blocks are added. It is important to know and identify the cornerstone of your business. Think of your cornerstone as the core principle that all other subsequent principles will be built on. If your chief cornerstone is money, then everything you do

should be built upon making, spending, saving, and receiving money. If your chief cornerstone is about relationships, then everything you do should be about creating, developing, maintaining, and keeping relationships.

The Scriptures tell us that the household of God was built on the foundation of the apostles and prophets, Christ being the Chief Cornerstone. If Christ is the Chief Cornerstone of your business, then all the other building blocks should align with the principles taught in His Word.

"This is the stone which was rejected by you builders, which has become the Chief Cornerstone." -Psalm 118:22; Acts 4:11

Building Blocks

Once you've identified the chief cornerstone of your business, it's time to assemble the building blocks. Core principles are among some of the building blocks of your business. They are what you stand on as a business owner no matter what adversity you are faced with. Your core principles help identify the guidelines of how you operate your business, manage your staff and relate to your clients. Here are some examples of what a few core principles might be...

Honesty: Being forthright with your staff and clients about the true state of things, without hypocrisy.

Humbleness: Actions and attitudes that reflect humble behavior, operating without pride or presumption.

Trustworthiness: Operating with integrity that clients can trust in; do what you said and follow through.

Diligence: Persistent effort to complete the task at hand with superiority and excellence.

Commitment: Dedicated to the greater good of the company, staff or client in lieu of oneself.

What Are Your Core Principles?

Write down trigger-words that describe the principles you want your staff or clients to experience within your establishment. What are some of the keywords that describe the values you intend to operate within your business relationships? What core principles do you want others to remember about you, your staff, and your business?

Using A Plumb Line

The plumb line is among the most simple yet the most accurate tool in determining the exactness of a vertical line. It consists of a weight or plummet suspended from a string using the natural law of gravity to determine vertical accuracy. It's a picture of the exactness and accuracy of God's Word as the true plumb line.

Aligning your life to the plumb line of God's Word is the responsibility of all believers. Though you may never measure up perfectly straight, that does not release you from faithing in the One who does, the perfect Son of God. His persecutions and temptations, His suffering and triumphs, His rejection and victories are all recorded in one Book that you might have a plumb line for your life. Every word of God is pure; it is inspired, infallible, tested and true. The Bible is perfectly complete and It is the true plumb line for which all things are measured!

"Behold, the Lord stood on a wall made with a plumb line, with a plumb line in His hand. And the Lord said to me, 'Amos, what do you see?' And I said, 'A plumb line.' Then the Lord said: 'Behold, I am setting a plumb line In the midst of My people Israel.' " - Amos 7:7-8

Misalignment

What happens when things get out of alignment? Often misalignments start with the smallest infractions that lead to greater mishaps. The Leaning Tower of Pisa is a great example of this misalignment. Without multiple corrective reconstructions on the Tower, it likely would have collapsed centuries ago! Business relationships work the same way. The smallest miscommunication left ignored or undone can lead to damaging and destructive results. Whether you are dealing with a staff member or a client, it is crucial to take the time to resolve even the smallest matters early before they become so far off track that you soon have a train wreck in your midst.

There is an undeniable principle of small things. The small things done right over time can make a business, and the small things left ignored or undone over time can break a business. This applies to actions as well as attitudes. The seemingly small things that don't align with the plumb line can soon become a twelve-foot tilt when not corrected.

How about the incident between King David and Bathsheba? (2 Samuel 11) What started as a small glance from David's rooftop, lead to an adulterous affair, a contract hit on Uriah's life, and the death of David's son. Just a little lustful look left unchecked soon turned into premeditated manslaughter.

King David got the conviction over what had happened, but not soon enough to keep his faithful servant, Uriah, alive. Even though David may have allowed a small thing to turn into a big thing in his relationship with Bathsheba, he still knew in order to get this right, his relationship had to be restored with the Lord first and foremost. David's heartfelt conviction brought godly repentance. Repentance that says...

"Create in me a clean heart, O God, and renew a steadfast spirit within me. Do not cast me away from your presence and do not take your Holy Spirit from me. Restore to me the joy of my salvation, and uphold me by Your generous Spirit. Then I will teach transgressors Your ways, and sinners shall be converted to You." -Psalm 51:10-13

In order to correct something, you must first be willing to confront it! The Prophet Nathan confronted King David about the sin, but the Lord corrected King David for the sin. Whether you are being confronted, or you are confronting others, there is always going to be correcting to do. It's a part of life, it's a part of relationships, and it's a part of doing business.

The Correction Process
So you've acknowledged something is out of alignment with the core principles you've set forth in your business, whether it's a staff member or a client, or even yourself, now it's time to confront it and correct it. One thing to know about correction...

Correction Always Goes Downstream, Never Upstream!
In other words, the subordinate does not correct his superior, in regards to position or authority within your establishment. Remember the example with King David? The prophet Nathan may have confronted King David, but

the Lord did the correcting. Sheep do not correct sheep, but the shepherd corrects the sheep. In the same manner, an Army Lieutenant does not correct his Captain, nor does his Captain correct his Commanding Major, and that same Major had certainly better not correct his Five-Star General. Correction always starts at the head and works its way down, not up and not sideways.

Now, if you are the one who needs correcting, be prepared to embrace the paddle, for God's correction on your life and in your faith-based company is going to be a lot tougher than man's correction. But, whom the Father loves, He corrects.

"Embrace the paddle. Kiss the Son." -Psalm 2:12

"My son, do not despise the chastening of the Lord, nor be discouraged when you are rebuked by Him; for whom the Lord loves He chastens, and scourges every son whom He receives. If you endure chastening, God deals with you as with sons; for what son is there whom a father does not chasten? Now no chastening seems to be joyful for the present, but painful; nevertheless, afterward it yields the peaceable fruit of righteousness to those who have been trained by it." -Hebrews 12:5-7 + 11

There is no best way to bring correction to your staff, except with sincerity and truth. Sometimes it may require a firm upper hand, other times a gentle corrective word will do. If the offense has been repeated even after documented warnings, you may need to send them home for a week without pay and let God convict them and sort it out. As each situation varies, you'll need to work it out yourself with fear and trembling.

If you let it, this is when the plumb line of God's Word can guide you through what to do, how to do it, and when to do it. We guarantee there is a revealing story to align with any and every situation you will go through. There is still nothing new under the sun that hasn't already been done before, and His Word still holds all the answers you'll need.

Unheard Construction
It's amazing to think that during the construction of Solomon's temple, not one tool was heard in the temple while it was being built, not even a hammer hitting a single nail. What does that tell us about relationships?

There is a time and place for certain things to be heard, or in this case not to be heard.

> "And the temple, when it was being built, was built with stone finished at the quarry, so that no hammer or chisel or any iron tool was heard in the temple while it was being built."
>
> - 1 Kings 6:7

When building a business, there will always be construction along the way, especially in the foundational stages. Be attentive to know what ears are listening to the construction of your business, of yourself and of your staff. Some things just aren't meant for all ears to hear.

Clients are not interested in hearing you and your staff work out the details of who's working what shift or who's taking vacation time or who's out sick. Nor do they need to publicly hear about disciplinary actions regarding their favorite associate. This is the kind of construction that is to be done behind the scenes, or as Solomon would put it, "Finish that stuff at the quarry, not at the temple site." In other words, handle it in the break room, not the front entry.

Think about it, construction sites are noisy, messy and often chaotic. Even the simplest jackhammer in use can drive a person mad by the end of the day. When it comes to figuring out the details of your business, keep that noise away from the serenity of your clients. They've come to patronize your business, not be antagonized by your business details.

Overhead Covering
Seldom will you find a home built without a roof overhead. It's main purpose: to cover and to protect. The same holds true for you, as the entrepreneur, the business owner and the chief executive officer. You are the covering for your business. This means covering and protecting your establishment, your staff and those under the authority of your faith-based company. The

greater the position, the greater the responsibilities, and with higher levels come higher devils. In other words, as the covering, you'll experience the storm at a much greater level than those who are sheltered under the protection of a trustworthy roof. But rest assured you're not in the storm alone when Christ is your covering.

Trust & Obedience

These are two of the key factors concerning a true covering. They apply in the natural sense as well as the spiritual sense. For example, in the midst of a torrential downpour, you trust that the roof over your head will keep you dry and safe from the pouring rain. That trust is only activated when obedience is added to it. You must obey by coming under the roof for protection. To trust that the covering will protect you while you continue to stand in the rain avails you nothing. The act of trusting requires the action of obedience, without which you truly have neither one.

It is the same application for the covering of a faith-based company. Employees, staff and clients alike must be able to trust you. They want to trust that what you say you will do, you actually do. Operating in a genuine spirit of justness, mercy, and humbleness (Micah 6:8) will develop a trust in your staff and clientele that generates obedience. The Scriptures are packed full of covering examples, including those to be emulated and those not so worthwhile to follow. Let's compare the two.

A True Covering

A true covering is like that of a true shepherd. He cares for and protects his flock. Take, for example, the shepherds of the Near East; they are responsible to watch out for the enemies that try to attack their sheep. They are continually defending the sheep from attackers and healing the wounded and sick sheep. These shepherds must also find and save lost or trapped sheep, showing them love and earning their trust. Hmmm, this sounds a lot like the parable in John chapter 10, verses 11-15...

"I am the good shepherd. The good shepherd gives His life for the sheep. But a hireling, he who is not the shepherd, one who does not own the sheep, sees the wolf coming and leaves the sheep and flees; and the wolf catches the sheep and scatters them. The hireling flees because he is a hireling and does not care about the sheep. I am the Good Shepherd; and I know My sheep, and am known by My own. As the Father knows Me, even so I know the Father; and I lay down My life for the sheep." -Matthew 5:10-12

As a "Business Shepherd," you have a responsibility to protect and care for those under your covering. Do not be fooled or intimidated by the wolves lurking about that seek to steal, to kill, and to destroy what you are doing. The world hates and resists those who are willing to lift up the name of Jesus Christ in the business arena. But find comfort knowing, "Blessed are those who are persecuted for righteousness sake."

It's important to understand a few things about sheep: They are at their best when they feel protected and safe from harm's way. Sheep become easily stressed without restful pastures and plenty of food and water. To the business shepherd, this means scheduling hours that allow proper recoup time between shifts. Proper nutrition consists not only of the paycheck that feeds them, but also of the words, actions, and attitudes that encourage and feed their souls. A good business shepherd must also be willing to correct the sheep when they go astray, lest they lead the rest of the flock off the cliff with them.

Sheep will trust a shepherd who has the ability to protect, nurture, and lead with confidence. The relationship between the Father and the Son in the above Scripture provides a model for the relationship between the shepherd and his sheep, and is an example worth emulating for the faith-based business owner.

Sometimes Seeing Is Believing

Although faith is the substance of things hoped for, and the evidence of things not seen, (Hebrews 11:1) sometimes people just want and need to see things firsthand for themselves. When a client can see the unique trust and godly obedience between a true business shepherd and his associates it generates a different and greater level of trust between the client and your establishment. It is easier to put trust in someone whom you see others already trusting, than to go it alone. Clients want to know you are trustworthy before they trust you. It is a bit of an oxymoron.

What character traits should your faith-based company exhibit? You be the judge. Here is a hint for finding some of the traits that the Lord looks for in a trustworthy business... Proverbs 3:5-6; 1 Samuel 15:22-23; Romans 1:16-17; Micah 6:8; Matthew 5:3-10, 9:12-13; James 4:6; John 13:34-35, and Acts 20:35.

A False Covering

A false covering is like a roof full of holes. When the sun is shining everything seems fine, however when the rains come, watch out for the leaks! The intentions of discussing the false covering is not so that you can point the finger at someone else, but so that you can identify the shortcomings in your own business and realign them according to your convictions and according to God's Word.

False coverings come like thieving wolves. Their presumptuous pride will steal just about anything. Their favorite thefts include: stealing positions, power, peace, time, life, spouses, reputations, and mental and emotional ambitions. That pretty much concludes the top 10 "Do Not's" that God gave Moses on Mount Sinai.

Understand, this isn't about your neighbor's business; it's about acknowledging the seemingly petty theft in your own business. Theft, whether venial or grand, is a result of the perpetual state of sin that man is born into. Thankfully, there is an advocate to the Father in a perpetual state of intercession for that sin. So, should we keep on sinning? Certainly not!

The difference between the true and the false covering is not in the sin itself, but how they respond to the sin. A true covering will acknowledge, repent, turn, and learn from it, and teach others to do the same. The false covering has no such experience, but continues in the desires of his own flesh, leading his staff on a dead end relationship road to destruction.

"The thief does not come except to steal, and to kill, and to destroy. I have come that they may have life, and that they may have it more abundantly."
-John 10:10

CHAPTER SIX:
The Peculiar Advantage

Standing out from the crowd is essential in today's marketplace. What makes you and your business different from the rest? Being a little peculiar is not only a good thing; it's a God thing! It means to set oneself exclusively apart from all others by distinction and by one's own unique features. This is exactly how God's Word describes His chosen people. Those who have stepped out of darkness and into the light are considered His special treasure. The original Greek language translates it as a "peculiar" people. God has made a distinct difference in those whom He has chosen for Himself, and even the world can clearly differentiate this truth. In like manner, your service needs to be differentiated and peculiar among all others.

Throughout this chapter we will be covering what it takes to have a peculiar advantage. There is a distinct advantage when you have differentiating service with client correlation in your business. We will also discuss creating a business slogan that aligns with your banner Scripture and vision statement and lastly, name recognition.

"For you are a holy people to the Lord your God; the Lord your God has chosen you to be a peculiar people for Himself, a special treasure above all the peoples on the face of the earth." -Deuteronomy 7:6

"But you are a chosen generation, a royal priesthood, a holy nation, a peculiar people, that you may proclaim the praises of Him who called you out of darkness into His marvelous light." -Matthew 7:15

Differentiating Service

It is a key element in relationship building. In essence, it is the difference between something common and something extraordinary. A common business relationship is like that of a common acquaintance that is to know someone or something slightly. It is somewhat indifferent and unattached. Now, on the other hand differentiating service is that which is extra ordinary, different than the rest, unique and peculiar in it's own special way. Good or bad, people notice those things that are different.

Take for example, John the Baptist. If he had just continued in his father's footsteps as a priest, he might not have received too much attention. But, John was different. He clothed himself with camel's hair and wore a leather belt around his waist (an interesting outfit even in those days); and his food was locusts and wild honey (Matthew 3:4). What he ate was peculiar and what he spoke was peculiar. But, with peculiarity arises curiosity.

"In those days John the Baptist came preaching in the wilderness of Judea, and saying, 'Repent, for the kingdom of heaven is at hand!'... Then Jerusalem, all Judea, and all the region around the Jordan went out to him and were baptized by him in the Jordan, confessing their sins." -Matthew 3:1-2 & 5-6

John's message drew a crowd. Both those who agreed and those who opposed him gathered to hear what he had to say. This is an advertising campaign worth mimicking. Like John, not all will want to buy what you are selling, but really just getting them through the door is the first challenge. Peculiar and unique may get their attention, but what you do next will either gather or scatter their attention. This is called client correlation.

To differentiate means to set your service apart from all others by distinction and by its own unique features and characteristics.

Take for example; if you have ever traveled to Phoenix, Arizona, you probably discovered that besides being one of the seemingly hottest places in America, it is a retail center paradise. There are dozens of shops on almost every other corner. It's really a bit unbelievable. As a consumer, it is great. As a business owner, it means a lot of competition. When it comes to food choices there are so many options in every food category that you could dine out for years and not hit the same place twice.

Choices Galore
Regarding the slew of restaurant choices in Phoenix, if you want Asian food, you can choose from: Tokyo Express, Shogun Express, Oriental Express, Kyoto Bowl, New China Buffet, China Place, Little Tokyo, P.F. Chang's Bistro, Bamboo Grill, and the list goes on and on.

With all these choices, what makes a person choose one establishment over another? Is it that one has better rice, or a better atmosphere, or a better choice of entrees? Or does fine quality and fantastic service set them apart? These are questions you'll need to answer about your own business.

Client Correlation
So, by now you may be able to differentiate, but can you correlate? Correlation is the process of establishing a relationship or orderly connection between two or more items.

A good example of correlation would be the relationship between the Old Testament and the New Testament. It is possible for each to stand alone, but together they create the full counsel of God. For the Old Testament conceals what is written in the New Testament, and the New Testament has the Old Testament revealed out of it. Only together can they create the perfect correlation in every sense of the word.

In business, to correlate means to align your service or product with a clearly defined and understood market niche. Regardless of how tough the competition may seem, it has little bearing if you correlate effectively. Let's say for example, you have discovered that in your area there are a large number of homes with stone flooring. This is a niche market that will require a professional system to clean and maintain. Starting a business that specializes in stone cleaning and restoration would be a fantastic correlation to this need. Identify the specific need and accommodate it with professional uniqueness.

Keep in mind that correlation is never to be in a static state, but rather a perpetual state of movement. As the market, environment, or economy changes, be ready and willing to shift with it. This does not mean dropping your values or loosing sight of the vision God has given you for your company, but simply moving forward by faith with flexibility. Godly flexibility means to flex with God's plans in lieu of your own, not compromising His agenda in lieu of man's ideals.

Let's look at a few correlation and differentiation attempts made by some well-known brands.

Avis: "We Try Harder"
Bounty: "The Quicker Picker Upper"
Burger King: "Have It Your Way"
KFC: "Finger Lickin' Good"
State Farm: "Like A Good Neighbor, State Farm Is There"
American Express: "Never Leave Home Without It"

Each of these examples involves a niche correlation between the client and service offered by that specific business. They have each made a specific statement about their unique service within their slogan that sets them apart from their competition. Not only does it set them apart, but it also draws the attention of specific clients with specific wants and needs to patronize their establishment.

The best way to truly correlate with your customer is to make it personal. Do you suppose that when Bounty released their new paper towel, it had something to do with the fact that someone in the establishment personally wanted a stronger paper towel that could quickly pick up a spill without having to use half the roll to do it? They identified a need that was personal to them and then took it public. This is what we call successful correlation.

CONSUMER: You have what I want

PROVIDER: I have what you need

Correlation In The Scriptures

The writer of 2 Chronicles (2:3-10,12-16) lays out a great example of a custom fit relationship between a "provider" and a "consumer" that uses the same correlation principles discussed herein.

King Solomon's Letter To Hiram king Of Tyre...

"As you have dealt with David my father, and sent him cedars to build himself a house to dwell in, so deal with me. Behold, I am building a temple for the name of the Lord my God, to dedicate it to Him, to burn before Him sweet incense, for the continual showbread, for the burnt offerings morning and evening, on the Sabbaths, on the New Moons, and on the set feasts of the Lord our God. This is an ordinance forever to Israel. And the temple which I build will be great, for our God is greater than all gods. But who is able to build Him a temple, since heaven and the heaven of heavens cannot contain Him? Who am I then, that I should build Him a temple, except to burn sacrifice before Him? Therefore send me at once a man skillful to work in gold and silver, in bronze and iron, in purple and crimson and blue, who has skill to engrave with the skillful men who are with me in Judah and Jerusalem, whom David my father provided. Also send me cedar and cypress and algum logs from Lebanon, for I know that your servants have skill to cut timber in Lebanon; and indeed my servants will be with your servants, to prepare timber for me in abundance, for the temple which I am about to build shall be great and wonderful. And indeed I will give to your servants, the woodsmen who cut timber, twenty thousand kors of ground wheat, twenty thousand kors of barley, twenty thousand baths of wine, and twenty thousand baths of oil."

King Hiram's Response To King Solomon...

"Blessed be the Lord God of Israel, who made heaven and earth, for He has given King David a wise son, endowed with prudence and understanding, who will build a temple for the Lord and a royal house for himself! And now I have sent a skillful man, endowed with understanding, Huram my master craftsman (the son of a woman of the daughters of Dan, and his father was a man of Tyre), skilled to work in gold and silver, bronze and iron, stone and wood, purple and blue, fine linen and crimson, and to make any engraving and to accomplish any plan which may be given to him, with your skillful men and with the skillful men of my lord David your father. Now therefore, the wheat, the barley, the oil, and the wine which my lord has spoken of, let him send to his servants. And we will cut wood from Lebanon, as much as you need; we will bring it to you in rafts by sea to Joppa, and you will carry it up to Jerusalem."

King Hiram has the finest of cedar and cypress trees in abundance. His men are highly skilled craftsman, engravers, metal smiths and planning engineers. Hiram has a niche product and service that is practically custom fit to the needs, wants, and desires of King Solomon. Now, if he can just consummate the deal, he's got it made!

Business Slogans
We touched a little bit on slogans in the previous correlation examples, but let's dive in a little deeper.

What Is A Slogan?
A slogan is considered a short and memorable phrase often used in advertising. Interestingly enough, the origin of the word slogan is derived from "sluagh," which means army plus "gairm," which means shout. It originated as the historical Scottish war cry. Hmm, interesting indeed! So your slogan is really the war cry for your business, a call made to rally others together for a specific campaign. And, that specific campaign is for others to do business with your establishment.

The business slogan that you choose should hold many of the same attributes as your company name, company logo, banner Scripture and vision statement. It should tell something about who you are, what you represent, what you offer and what sets you apart from the crowd. It should be short, catchy and easy to remember.

Let's look at a few popular slogans for inspiration. Take a look at the slogans below. What instantly jumps into your mind?

"It keeps going, and going, and going..."
"They're grrrreat!"
"Plop, plop, fizz, fizz, oh what a relief it is."

If these companies have done a successful job with consistent and deliberate communication, you should be thinking: Energizer Batteries, Kellogg's Frosted Flakes, and Alka-Seltzer.

Notice that the slogan often invokes two things. First, it is a reminder that they cater to a specific target niche. For example, the slogan used by Energizer Batteries, "They keep going, and going, and going..." is directed toward the economy market and the longevity of their product. Secondly, it's a statement of differentiation. Quizno's opened with the slogan, "Mmmm toasty!" This simple element of differentiation has now forced Subway to toast their sandwiches also! This is an excellent reminder that differentiation is never static, but evolving with the demands and desires of the consumer, without loosing it's origin. Slogans should have consistency to them, but they may change as you and your company grows and changes.

One more thing, it is a general statistic that advertising slogans that involve humor are among the most favored and well known. Just look at the three used in our previous examples, each has a touch of humor to them.

Take time to brainstorm a few slogan ideas. Remember to draw from the foundations that you have already laid with your logo, banner Scripture or vision statement.

Name Recognition

By this point in the program, you should already have chosen a name for your business. If not, review "The Naming Process" in chapter two. A successful business name is one that is catchy, memorable, and most of all, one that represents your business and what you do.

Now it's time to take that name a step further and consider how to get it recognized. Without further ado, let's look at the greatest and most recognized name in history, a name that is above all names... Jesus Christ.

"Therefore God also has highly exalted Him and given Him the name which is above every name, that at the name of Jesus every knee should bow, of those in heaven, and of those on earth, and of those under the earth, and that every tongue should confess that Jesus Christ is Lord, to the glory of God the Father." -Philippians 2:9-11

Before we move into how to get your name recognized, let's take a side bar and review some of the names that our Lord has become recognized as.

GOD HAS HIGHLY EXALTED HIM &
GIVEN HIM A NAME ABOVE ALL NAMES

GENESIS: The Beginning & The Seed
EXODUS: The Deliverer
LEVITICUS: The High and Holy Moral Code
NUMBERS: Pillar of Cloud by Day/ Fire by Night
DEUTERONOMY: The Prophet Just Like Moses
JOSHUA: The Strategist / Captain of the Host
JUDGES: The Jawbone of a Donkey
RUTH: God Almighty / Kinsman Redeemer
1 & 2 SAMUEL: Ebenezer / Stone of Help
1 & 2 KINGS: The Lord of History
1 & 2 CHRONICLES: The God of Accountability
EZRA: The Priest / The God-Father
NEHEMIAH: The Rebuilder of Broken Walls
ESTHER: The Mordecai at the Gates
JOB: The Slayer / Dayspring Fountain
PSALM: The Good Shepherd
PROVERBS / ECCLECIASTES: Wisdom
SONG OF SOLOMON: Rose of Sharon / Lilly of the Valley
ISAIAH / JEREMIAH: The Prince of Peace / Righteous Branch
LAMENTATIONS: The Weeping Prophet
EZEKIEL: The All-Seeing Wheel / Restorer
DANIEL: The Forth Man in the Fiery Furnace
HOSEA/JOEL/AMOS/OBADIAH: The God of Judgment
JONAH / MICAH: The God of Compassion
NAHUM / HABAKKUK: The God of Destruction / Embracing Father
ZEPHANIAH: The Hiding God
HAGGAI: The God of Teamwork / Unity
ZECHARAIH / MALACHI: Immanuel - God With Us
MATHEW: The Messiah
MARK: The Wonder Worker
LUKE: The Son of Man
JOHN: The Son of God
ACTS: Pentecost in the Upper Room
ROMANS: The Justifier
1 & 2 CORINTHIANS: The Gifts of the Spirit

GALATIANS:	The Lord of Liberty
EPHESIANS:	The Lord of Riches
PHILIPPIANS:	The God of Joy & Peace
COLOSSIANS:	The Fullness of the Godhead Bodily
1 & 2 THESSALONIANS:	The Returning Christ
1 & 2 TIMOTHY:	The Mediator Between God & Man
TITUS:	The Lord of Responsibility & Order
PHILEMON:	El Shaddai - More Than Enough
HEBREWS:	The High Priest
JAMES:	The Great Physician
1 & 2 PETER:	The Blessed Promise
1 & 2 & 3 JOHN:	Everlasting Love
JUDE:	The Divine Preserver
REVELATIONS:	King of Kings & Lord of Lords

As you look at the different names of our Lord throughout the Scriptures, you'll find they are more than mere titles, but they embody the full onama character of Christ. Each of these names represents who Christ is and how He is known. His widespread recognition isn't just because of the name that He was given, but because of who He is and what He accomplished, that accomplishment being His incarnation, crucifixion, resurrection and glorification!

What & Who Of Recognition
In the realm of the faith-based company, we define recognition as: A company whose name, products, or services are recognized, acknowledged and identified by what they represent and who they are associated with.

What: (i.e.) Christ was recognized by the things He did and the things He said.

Who: (i.e.) Christ was recognized because of His identification to the Father.

The simple fact that you are known by the Lord gives you that peculiar advantage that we spoke about previously in this chapter. That old saying, "It's all about who you know" can certainly be applied here. When your relationship with Him is evidenced in what you think, do, and say, it draws the attention of others. This is the kind of recognition that sets you apart from the rest of the crowd. It creates a relationship between your business and the client that impresses them to want to know you better. In other words, what they are saying about your establishment is, "There is something different here, I want to experience this again."

Acknowledgement And Recognition
The difference between basic acknowledgement and name recognition has a lot to do with repetition. Take for example King David, one of the most well known men in the Bible besides Christ Himself. Was he so well known because of his great military exploits, or his inspiring psalms, or because he had a heart after God's own heart? Or do you suppose you recognize his name because it is mentioned over 1,100 times in the Scriptures, more than any other individual throughout God's entire Word?

What about Josheb-Basshebeth, who killed 800 men at one time, and was the first mentioned of David's mighty men? Do you recognize his name? Or how about Ethan the Ezrahite, who so eloquently wrote of God's mercies, faithfulness and everlasting covenant in the 89th Psalm? Do you recall his name? Or maybe you might recognize the name Rizpah, whose godly heart posture was seen in her selfless acts after the sacrificial death of her sons to make amends with the Gibeonites. What they did and whom they represented are worth recognizing, but without repetition, they often become easily forgotten. We'll talk more about repetition as we move into the subject of communication in the next chapter.

Q: Now that you have a general understanding of whom and for what your business shall be recognized; what should you do to obtain this name recognition?

A: The answer is relatively simple: Identify those in the Scriptures that received recognition worth obtaining and mimic the same principles in your own business. God's inspired Word was written and recorded for our admonition. In effect, it is our game tapes and ultimate playbook. With that said, let's move ahead to a few worthy examples.

"For whatever things were written before were written for our learning, that we through the patience and comfort of the Scriptures might have hope."
-Romans 15:4

Model Recognition: King David

But the house of David grew stronger and stronger (2 Samuel 3:1). Why? Because David had a heart after God's own heart (Acts 13:22). He sought the Lord for direction. He fled to Christ for refuge. He heeded the voice of the prophets. He knew the value of praise and worship. And more than anything else, David had an unchangeable belief in the faithful and forgiving nature of God. He was a man who lived with great zeal, and like you and I, a man who sinned, but David was quick to confess his sins. His confessions were from the heart, and his repentance was genuine. David never took God's forgiveness lightly or his blessings for granted. The Hebrews writer recognizes David in the "Hall of Faith," listed among those who through faith subdued kingdoms, worked righteousness, obtained promises, stopped the mouths of lions, quenched the violence of fire, escaped the edge of the sword, out of weakness were made strong, became valiant in battle, and turned to flight the armies of the aliens (Hebrews 11:32-34).

Indeed, all of these traits and more brought godly recognition to King David. Emulating King David begins with having the heart of King David (aka the heart of God). Ezekiel puts it this way, "Then I will give them one heart, and I will put a new spirit within them, and take the stony heart out of their flesh and give them a heart of flesh, that they may walk in My statues and keep My judgments and do them; and they shall be My people, and I will be their God." (Ezekiel 11:19-20)

This spiritual and moral transformation is not something that we do; it is something that we receive. The Father says those who ask according to His will shall receive, and those who seek will find, and to those who knock, it will be opened to them. So, ask, seek, and knock according to His perfect will that He would give you His choice gift of the Holy Spirit, and that your heart would be that of the heart of God.

Model Recognition: Elijah
Without a doubt, Elijah is among the most well known of the prophets. His legendary recognition is shown at the great transfiguration on the mountaintop along with Moses as they speak with Christ. In both appearance and in spirit, Peter, James, and John all recognize Elijah as a valid representation of the prophets. Elijah's single-minded commitment to God shocks and challenges us. His personal relationship with the Lord is seen in his set apart life and devotion to God's call on his life. Among the many miracles the Lord performed through Elijah, the show down at Mount Carmel is certainly one of the most spectacular.

By now, you may be thinking it's unlikely that you'll be transfigured into a glowing being at the top of a mountain, or have a water drenched burnt offering suddenly ignite before the enemies of God. So what does this have to do with your business relationships? Well, everything! It's time to put those spiritual glasses back on as we look at the example that Elijah sets for the businessman or woman in this drama on the stage of history.

It's important to understand that everything that happens at Mount Carmel is part of the key plot to reveal that, "The Lord, He is God!" (1 Kings 18:20-40) Elijah has a point to prove and a case to win, for he faithfully knows the truth of the outcome. This is the same confidence that the faith-based business owner should walk in regarding his business, his service and his products. It does not matter that there are 850 businesses to your 1, when God is fighting on your side of the battle. Like Elijah, there are going to be times when you feel alone, and you're the only one left in this world willing to lift up the name of Jesus in your business, but rest assured, "There are 7000 whose knees have not bowed to Baal." (1 Kings 19:18). Follow Elijah's example when it comes to defeating the competition. Be ready and willing to let them go first. Elijah told the false prophets, you call on the name of your gods, and I'll call on the name of the Lord, and the God who answers wins. So they did "their thing" but to no avail. Then it was Elijah's turn, and he even raised the stakes by drenching his offering with water. Elijah prayed and the Lord heard him and consumed the offering with fire.

You Go First
When approaching a new client for business that claims they already have someone for the job, let him or her know what or how you can beat and improve on the competition. Let's say you had an amazing patented-technology cleaning system. Can you assert enough confidence in your system to say to your prospect, "What time will your current company come to clean? Let them come as usual and then I'll come and re-clean right after them, and then you'll be able to see the true difference for yourself." We've coined this the, "You Go First Method" against the competition. In the spirit of Elijah, you're likely to have victory with a winning product and winning service! As the old saying goes, sometimes it's good to save the best for last.

Model Recognition: Paul
Who was once recognized as the leading persecutor of the church became one of the most influential voices in all the New Testament. The apostle Paul led a challenging life sandwiched between two worlds, that of his prominent and devout Jewish upbringing, and that of his transformed belief and life in Jesus Christ as the promised Messiah to the Jews and the Gentiles alike. If you've ever been stuck between a rock and hard spot, you might have an idea of what this meant.

Paul had the unveiling task of preaching the true gospel of Christ that Jesus came, not contrary to the law, but as the ultimate fulfillment of the law. This indeed was no easy task, but rather one full of persecution and sacrifice, triumphs and joys. The Damascus Road experience left Paul with the profound revelation that the God whom he had been serving, he had also radically misunderstood. For Paul, the impossible had now become reality and he would never again be the same. All of Paul's future actions and attitudes now become a direct result of the up close and personal relationship he now has with Jesus Christ through His Holy Spirit.

The Responsibility Factor

Businessman or businesswoman, have you had that Damascus Road experience yet? Were you once blind, but now you see? That unveiled truth comes with a responsibility, a personal one and a public one! Personally: it's about the relationship you now have in Him, as He abides in you and you in Him. Publicly: it's about the call to share that same truth with others.

The Scriptures tell us Paul made a living as a tent maker. Do you suppose he only spoke about Christ in the Synagogues, or do you think he shared the gospel with those in his business dealings? You have a unique opportunity now just as Paul did then. Paul took advantage of the opportunity to share the Good News message with prominent businessmen and women, people of power and influence. Some scorned and stoned him, but others were persuaded and believed (Acts 17:4 & 12). When Paul writes, "Imitate me as I imitate Christ," consider his boldness to share the gospel in the business arena as a great place to start.

"For though you might have ten thousand instructors in Christ, yet you do not have many fathers; for in Christ Jesus I have begotten you through the gospel. Therefore I urge you, imitate me. For this reason I have sent Timothy to you, who is my beloved and faithful son in the Lord, who will remind you of my ways in Christ, as I teach everywhere in every church. Imitate me, just as I also imitate Christ." -1 Corinthians 4:15-17 & 11:1

CHAPTER SEVEN:
Communication Protocol

Share & Share Alike

Communication in a simple nutshell is all about sharing, the sharing of information, ideas, time, talents and treasures. The word commune is derived from the Greek word "koinonia," which is often translated as fellowship, communication or sharing. It is the essence of what the church was founded on at Pentecost as noted in Acts 2:40-47.

Communication that results from koinonia fellowship is centered on a spirit of giving that lines up with where your heart and treasures is. Godly communication and generous sharing is one way to store up for yourself treasures in heaven where moth and rust do not destroy and where thieves do not break in and steal. (Matthew 6:19-21) Koinonia communication is not a one-time event, but an ongoing steadfastness and development of sharing through giving and receiving. This is the kind of communication the faith-based company ought to follow after.

"And they continued steadfastly in the apostles' doctrine and fellowship, in the breaking of bread, and in prayers." -Acts 2:42

Repetition: The School Master

Communication in the business realm means to consistently remind your customers why they chose you and why you remain their best choice! This ongoing reminder is the same precept the Lord laid out for us in the Holy Communion. Taking communion is about communing with the Creator of heaven and earth. It is about an active calling to mind who the Lord is and what He has done in and through your life. It is recalling why He chose you, and why He is still your best choice in response to that calling.

It's ongoing and perpetual, that's why the Lord said, "This do, as often as you drink it, in remembrance of Me." It is a statute forever and a perpetual form of communication and recognition between the believer and Christ until His return.

As a business owner, you need to create that same form of communication and recognition with your client that they might recall your business and it's benefits as it pertains to them until they return again to your establishment. To successfully do this, your communication must be consistent and deliberate. One way is through an effective slogan. When your slogan is repeated over and over again, in print advertising, on radio, in television commercials, on your website, through social media, and within in-store advertising and displays, it becomes a slogan that sticks.

A fantastic example of this "over and over again" gestalt approach is found throughout the Scriptures when God makes His slogan clear that, "The just shall live by faith." Here are just a few of His ads...

"For by grace you have been saved through faith, and that not of yourselves; it is the gift of God, not of works, lest anyone should boast." -Ephesians 2:8-9

"Therefore we conclude that a man is justified by faith apart from the deeds of the law." -Romans 3:28

"But the just shall live by faith." -Habakkuk 2:4, Romans 1:17, Hebrews 10:38

"Therefore having been justified by faith, we have peace with God through our Lord Jesus Christ." -Romans 5:1

"But without faith it is impossible to please Him, for he who comes to God must believe that He is, and that He is a rewarder of those who diligently seek Him." -Hebrews 11:6

The Gestalt Theory
Repetition is undoubtedly considered the school master by many. The more you hear something, the more likely you are to retain it. Our previous subject of faith is no exception. The apostle Paul puts it this way, "Faith

comes by hearing, and hearing by the Word of God." (Romans 10:17) Notice what tense Paul uses in this verse. It is not the past tense of heard but the ongoing perfect tense of hearing, something that is continually performed. Effective repetition is not mundane or humdrum, but when exercised correctly, it instills interest and peaks curiosity. Using the gestalt theory of repetition is considered among the most effective of methods.

ge·stalt
1.   An organized whole that is perceived as more than the sum of its parts

2.   Literally to form or shape using multiple methods or techniques

The term gestalt has become commonly known in the fitness industry as a method of physical training and conditioning. It is the concept of repeating similar yet different exercises multiple times for the same muscle from different angles. For example if a person wanted to build his bicep muscles, he might perform a bicep curl with a straight bar, with a curly bar, with dumb bells, also hammer curls or maybe isolated curls. All of these exercises work the same muscle group, but repeating the exercise through different angles and techniques produces a greater whole result than just one single exercise repeated over again without variation. Are you starting to get the picture of how this relates to communication in the business relationship?

Have you ever heard something said by a person that really didn't mean much to you, but then someone else came along and said the same thing but in a different way, and "kaboom" the lights suddenly came on for you? This is why gestalting is so important.

Communication is not limited to just what you say, but also how you say it. It likewise includes everything you do and how you do it. What and how you communicate to your prospective clients determines whether they will choose to do business with you or not. Think of the way you communicate a single idea to your client in the same way the athlete trains his bicep muscles. Create different, yet similar ways of communicating key points to your client through interesting and distinct repetitions.

Remind Clients Why They Chose You
It's important to communicate in different ways why and how your business and your service is superior to the other options your client has to choose from. Remember when we spoke about your core principles as the building blocks of your business?

Here is where you implement and decide how you are going to communicate those core principles and key values to your client. Let's look at a few communication methods delivered through superior customer service and the response they generate.

Prompt Recognition: Clients receive this as the first signal that their presence matters to you and excellent service is likely to follow.

Genuine Friendliness: People are quickly offended by rude or indifferent behavior, but they are quickly satisfied in a friendly environment.

Efficient Competency: People want to deal with experienced professionals. They may overlook simple mistakes but they don't forget blatant ignorance.

Punctual Speed: Clients want to know and feel that you are being efficient and prompt, yet not rushed, even when they may be taking their time.

Value Of Worth: Most clients look for quality that generates worth and value.

Undivided Integrity: Maintaining integrity that clients can trust in is the glue that will get customers to stick to you.

Maintained Cleanliness: Clients find peace and comfort in spaces that look clean and smell clean. People shun physical spaces that are not well maintained.

Prompt Follow-Up: Clients want and expect prompt responses to their needs and desires. Lack of which indicates that they don't matter to you.

Communication Attributes

Attributes are qualities or features regarded as a characteristic or inherent part of someone or something. The attributes of your business need to show through the way you communicate with others. Like it or not, as a business owner, you are under constant scrutiny and evaluation. Clients will use all their senses in the evaluation process of how well you have communicated with them and what you have attributed to them... what they see, what they smell, what they hear, what they feel, and sometimes what they taste. Have you measured up to their expectations, or even more so, have you measured up to your own expectations?

Poor Communication

Sometimes knowing what to do means knowing what not to do! When poor examples are set for clients, it leaves them with a poor impression. Poor impressions are poor for business! One thing to consider when addressing the "what-not's," is to be attentive to realize that they apply to everyone within your establishment. That includes you, your top paid executive, and your minimum wage part-timer.

For example, let's say a client walks in the door and you are too busy to greet him. Well, if everyone else did the same thing that you did, then no one would greet the client and he would feel as though his presence was of no importance to you or your establishment. You have now lost the first impression to sheer neglect. Rule #1: don't assume someone else will do what you are supposed to do; again this applies to everyone. If you can't get to them, then signal to another associate to cover for you. Small details left undone over time can turn into a mound of disasters that can ultimately break you without corrective measures. It's much better to be proactive than reactive when it comes to customer service.

Communication Sent: Message Received

It's time to take it to the other side of the spectrum and look at a few poor communication deliveries and the messages that are received by them.

Communication Sent: Lunch at fine dining restaurant - Food and service is great, but the restroom is filthy.

Message Received: Their kitchen is probably filthy also; maybe I won't come back lest I end up with a case of food poisoning.

Communication Sent: Hostess escorts you to your table, tosses the menu on the table, turns and walks away.

Message Received: Based on that greeting, I hate to see if the waitress is any better. My business must not be that important to them.

Communication Sent: Local dry cleaners - No greeting, no "thank you," and no verification of my ticket, but the shirts appear to be clean at first glance.

Message Received: If they don't pay any attention to politeness or basic details, maybe they won't pay attention to small stains that need extra attention either.

Communication Sent: Retail clothing store - You can't find your size, and the associate tells you they only keep the most popular sizes in stock.

Message Received: You have been humiliated, insulted, and treated as an oddball who doesn't fit in, you probably won't return.

Communication Sent: House cleaning company - The public areas look great, but the less noticeable areas are still covered with dust.

Message Received: If they only give attention to the most-seen areas and disregard the places people don't notice, what else do they do when they think people aren't looking?

Residual Relationships

A person only knows as much about you as you share with him. Getting to really know someone takes time. You can't possibly understand every detail of an individual on a first date! Some things can only be experienced through exposure, which again takes time and repeated interaction. This is the same way clients view a new business engagement. At first, they're totally excited, happy, and even somewhat euphoric, then when reality sinks in and they return to their level-headed thinking state, they become fact finders and investigators.

Earning a client's business is one thing, but what about retaining it? The Scriptures boldly speak out against adulterous one night stands, and so should you as it relates to your business. A one-time sale is not the backbone of a solid faith-based company. Residual business can certainly make or break a company. Are you ready for a serious relationship... because residual business requires residual communication?

Communication Follow-Up

72 Hours

Follow up communication can be performed in a number of different ways. A simple post card sent out within 72 hours of the clients first visit saying, "Thank you for your recent business..." is a great place to start. God's Word is packed full of many amazing things, good and bad that took place in that special 72-hour golden rule of time.

10 Days

Be prepared to send an additional message about your company within the next 10 days. This correspondence should tell something special about you and your company. It can reiterate something they may have already learned about you or your business on their first meeting, but it also needs to share something new. Consider it like your second date, and let them in on a few secrets, such as upcoming sales, promotions, or events. Ten days is how long Daniel fasted when he sought communication with the Lord for what he ought to do next.

21 Days

Next communication date is 21 days. Twenty-one is the simple mathematics of 7 x 3. Seven symbolizes God's spiritual perfection, three denotes His divine manifestation. Together they represent God's divine spiritual perfection and manifestation. It is said it takes 21 days to make or break a habit, in that time, see what divine manifestation God will make or break in your business as He matures it to His perfection.

40 Days

Next communication date is 40 days. Forty has always represented a time of testing in the Scriptures. Moses dwelt in Pharaohs courts 40 years, then he kept the flocks in Midian 40 years, then he spent 40 years wandering in the wilderness with the Israelites, not to mention the 40 days he spent on Mt Sinai. How about the 40 days Joshua spent spying out the Promised Land, or the 40 days Jesus endured the temptations of Satan. A lot can happen in 40 days. Don't miss this milestone opportunity of communication. Again, take the time to share something new and personal about your company with your client throughout your follow-up communications.

By the 40-day mark, you should now have communicated with your client either through postal mail, email, social media or phone in at least four different and individual occurrences. Is your relationship building with the client? Absolutely! Through diligent follow-up and genuine caring communication, you have established one very critical element to your client. They matter to you!

Keep a regular schedule of how and when you intend to keep your business in front of the client. As we said earlier, repetition is the school master, so keep reminding your clients of why they chose you and how their business matters to you.

Webster's defines "follow-up" as a continuation or repetition of something that has already been started, a piece of work that builds on or exploits the success of earlier work. Based on this, the follow-up communication should be just as impressive as the initial interaction. It is intended to build upon or exploit the success that was already started. To exploit something in a positive way is to make full use of and derive optimum benefit from that thing. For example, a company might exploit the new technology they recently uncovered, or a consumer might exploit the news of a fantastic sale they discovered at their favorite retail clothing store. This is exploitation in its pure form.

So how can you "wow" your client in follow-up correspondence? For starters when they return to your place of business, make a note to remember their name, and greet them by it when they come in. People love to know that you know them by name.

"But now, thus says the Lord, who created you, O Jacob, and He who formed you, O Israel: 'Fear not, for I have redeemed you; I have called you by your name; you are Mine.' " -Isaiah 43:1

Secondly, exercise communication though a spirit of giving. Christ set this example when He gave His all for us. How much more then should we fulfill the commandment He has given us to love one another as He has loved us. Just as Christ expressed His love through giving, so we ought to do the same!

Consider buying an assortment of gift cards to favorable establishments in your area, like restaurants or theaters or sporting events that you can freely give to your clients. When God has truly given you a heart that unmistakably knows it is better to give than to receive, then watch and see your business relationships flourish.

PILLAR 2:
SEED TIME & HARVEST

CHAPTER EIGHT:
Seeds & Sowing

The strongest business is started as a small idea or seed in the mind of an entrepreneur. After this, there comes a need to identify your product or service, your niche market, and your prospective clients. Then cultivate, plant, harvest, and tend to your ground carefully, and watch your business grow.

Seed Time & Harvest focuses on the spirit of giving and how to apply this precept in your business. Throughout the Scriptures the genuineness of the Spirit is proven by the way that you give. Christ's perfect example is shown in how He gave everything for our account through His life, His death, and His resurrection. How much more should we follow that example in a life of giving, both in our personal affairs and in our day-to-day business affairs? A faith-based company will do well to center its core values and operations on a spirit of giving.

There are many ways to demonstrate the act of giving, as you shall see as this topic unfolds in the pages to follow. In addition, this chapter will be covering how to identify good ground, where to plant seeds in your business that will reap a plentiful harvest, and understanding how to use good measure. You will also experience the traditional subjects of prospecting, networking, advertising, marketing, referrals, and repeat business brought to life from a Biblical perspective.

God's Covenant With Creation

Before we can apply the Seed Time and Harvest principle in the business realm, it is important to understand what it means in the natural realm as well as the spiritual realm. For starters let's look at what God says about Seed Time and Harvest as it relates to His covenant promise with all creation.

"While the earth remains, seed time and harvest, cold and heat, winter and summer, and day and night shall not cease." -Genesis 8:22

Although we refer to Seed Time & Harvest as a principle, it's more than that. It's a promise! For all the promises of God are yes, and in Him amen, to the glory of God through us. (2 Corinthians 1:20) In other words, we can stand on what He says as solid, sure, and true. God is not a man that He should lie, nor a son of man that He should repent. Has He said, and will He not do? Or, has He spoken, and will He not make it good? (Num 23:19)

You see this promise is a direct result and reflection of the faith of Noah. As soon as Noah and his family exited the ark after the great flood, the first thing that Noah did was build an altar and make a sacrifice to the Lord. His thankfulness of salvation was shown through the act and spirit of giving. The Lord received Noah's offering as a soothing aroma. It is after this scene in the stage of history that God then makes a promise to all creation that He will never again destroy the earth by water.

When God created the first living thing, He gave it the ability to grow and multiply. How? Through the seed. Your life began by the seed principle and every act that you've done since then has been by the seed principle. Whether good seeds or bad seeds, whether you were consciously aware of it or not, the fact still remains that life is full of sowing and reaping.

With all this sowing, understand that God has a due season for every seed that you plant. Keep in mind that His timing may not be your timing. For His thoughts are not our thoughts, nor are His ways our ways. Just keep sowing the seed of His promise by faith in the soil of His grace.

The Principle Of Seed Faith

The very heart of seed faith is about giving out of that which cost you something. Take for example, King David and the purchase of the threshing floor on Mount Moriah. Araunah told David that he would give him the threshing floor, the oxen, the wood and whatever else he needed to make an offering to the Lord.

However King David said to him "No, but I will surely buy it from you for a price; nor will I offer burnt offerings to the Lord my God with that which costs me nothing." So David bought the threshing floor, the oxen, and the whole field and made an offering to the Lord from his own sacrifice and it was pleasing to the Lord. (2 Samuel 24:18-25)

This threshing floor on Mount Moriah is the same place where Abraham offered Isaac (Genesis 22:2) and the location of King Solomon's temple (2 Chronicles 3:1). Undoubtedly, this was an appointed and special place that the Lord would use in the pages of His-Story.

David understood the principle of seed faith. It must come from that which God has placed in your own hands. Our giving to the Lord must bear these 3 qualities.

1. **It Should Be Your Best:** When you give God your best, His Word says you can expect the same in return. (Proverbs 3:9-10)

2. **You Should Give To God First**: The tithe belongs to the Lord. No exceptions. (Exodus 23:19)

3. **You Should Give Generously**: For the Lord loves a hilarious giver. "Freely you have received, freely give" (Matthew 10:8)

Faith Without Doubting
When you plant a seed, God changes the nature of that seed so that it has the power to become a plant. A tender shoot from a dry root can surge forth with such life that it can even push through a mountain of earth to make its way upward. Christ says your faith is like a seed. When you put your faith into action without doubting, God allows it to take on a new nature, allowing even the most miraculous to spring forth.

Regarding seed faith, God's Word says that to each of you He has given a measure of faith (Romans 12:3). It is resident within you, implanted in your bosom. Secondly, His Word says that faith comes by hearing and hearing by the Word of God. (Romans 10:17) Hearing and heeding His Word waters that seed within.

Thirdly, His Word says that as you apply your faith you shall see your daily needs met. How? By putting your faith into action. When you sow even the smallest mustard seed of your faith into an action of love and obedience, watch how God waters it and brings its increase. By faith, speak to your mountain and see the power of the Lord bring about its removal.

Give And It Will Be Given
One of the keys to spiritual breakthrough is found in Jesus' call to "Give, and it will be given to you." Financial obstacles often tempt you to give up, but instead God's Word calls you to give away. True ministry involves coming to terms with your human tendency to hold on and to clutch things to yourself, especially material belongings. Christ said to his disciples that unless a grain of wheat falls into the ground and dies, it remains alone, but if it dies, it produces much grain or much fruit (John 12:24).

Jesus was not only referring to His own death and resurrection, but He was also referring to the sacrifices that man would need to make in order to truly follow Him. Certain things in your flesh must die in order to produce life-changing fruit. The pathway of yielding up all to Him often calls you to give when you yourself may be in need. (2 Corinthians 8:1-4) It may seem counterproductive, but giving out of your own need is God's way of clearing the avenues for heaven's gates to open wide and pour out a blessing on, in and through your own life.

Christ's sacrificial death opened up a whole new way of giving. You can no longer sacrifice or pay your way into God's mercy or grace. Jesus has paid your debt in full on the cross at Calvary. "Tetelistai," it is finished; the sin debt is paid forever. Your giving then, is no longer a debt that you owe, but a seed that you sow!

"Give, and it will be given to you: good measure, pressed down, shaken together, and running over will be put into your bosom. For with the same measure that you use, it will be measured back to you." -Luke 6:38

God Has A Due Season
There is a due season for every seed that you plant! God has a timetable for every seed that you sow. His timetable may not always be your timetable. Sometimes the due season appears with a quick return. And,

sometimes it means a slow return that may take years or even a lifetime to fully experience.

"Do not be deceived, God is not mocked; for whatever a man sows, that he will also reap. For he who sows to his flesh will of the flesh reap corruption, but he who sows to the Spirit will of the Spirit reap everlasting life. And let us not grow weary while doing good, for in due season we shall reap if we do not lose heart. Therefore, as we have opportunity, let us do good to all, especially to those who are of the household of faith." -Galatians 6:7-10

God's Word has given you three promises that you can count on regarding His due season. One: God will cause a harvest to come from your seeds. Two: God is always on time, never early and never late. Three: Your harvest will be of the same nature for which it was sown. Good seeds bring a good harvest and bad seeds bring a bad harvest.

God's Word also tells you what you ought to do while you are waiting for those seeds to grow. One: You must refuse to become discouraged. Two: You must be determined to keep your faith alive and active. Three: You must give and keep on giving; to love and keep on loving, knowing that a harvest has been guaranteed.

Sowing To The Flesh
Let's take another look at the verse from Galatians, this time zeroing in not on the season, but on where the seeds are sown.

What you sow, how you sow it, and where you sow it plays a huge factor in the type of harvest you will reap from those seeds. Seeds sown to the flesh reap instant gratification but long term pain. Continuing to sow seeds into the world, the flesh, and the devil will only reap a harvest of corruption! Understand, to break the cycle of poor seed sowing, you must overcome and condemn the world. You must resist and cast out the devil, and you must crucify the lusts and desires of the flesh. How is this done? It is only by the faith of Jesus in you who overcomes the adversary. Know your pitfalls and identify the strongman that causes you to stumble. Discern quickly that thing which may begin as a natural thing, but when left unchecked, it moves into the sensual and then turns into something obsessive, compulsive, and even demonic.

For example, you might enjoy having a glass of wine after dinner with your spouse, seems harmless, right? Then it's going out for a drink after work, then it turns into multiple drinks with your seemingly conscienceless single friends at the bar. Then when that's not exciting enough, that old enticing and familiar spirit will draw you into the night clubs, and then... get the idea? When what starts as something natural, if it's not kept in check, it will checkmate you! It doesn't take much for the temptation of the flesh to lead to a corrupted life. Keep your foot on the neck of the enemy, lest it take hold of you and your business. Don't be fooled into thinking your personal affairs have no bearing on your business. God holds the faith-based company more accountable than that.

Your flesh loves the satisfaction of its own flesh. Sowing the littlest seeds in the ground of temptation is like adopting a cute, tiny, little baby alligator that grows up and turns into a fire breathing dragon in your own home. It's dangerous for you personally, as well as detrimental and costly for your business. Regardless of how much Scripture you have read or memorized, God has given you a conscience. Let that be your guide! As you mature in Christ, your conscience will catch up with the convictions in God's Word (James 3:13-16 & 4:1-7; 1 Corinthians 6:12).

Universal Laws
Universal laws refer to those things that are known as universally true, verified without exceptions, and capable of being presented in a mathematical way. The most commonly known, without a doubt, is gravity. It's common knowledge that when you toss something of weight into the air, it's sure to fall to the ground; what goes up must come down. Everyone in life is sure to have a testimony about learning the lesson of gravity.

Among the other well-known universal laws are: the law of attraction and the law of increase. Both of which, center on the natural laws of reciprocity, or the direct relationship between two distinct objects. We'll expand on this as we move through the following pages. Let's start by looking at a few examples you are probably already familiar with.

If you play with fire... You're going to get burned! Water will always find... Its own level! You are what you... Eat!

The Law Of Attraction
The law of attraction could be simply stated as "like spirits attract like spirits." If you have any doubts about this, ask the drug addict if it is true.

Any so-called junkie can spot another junkie a mile away, almost as if there were some mysterious sonar radar working on his behalf. In the same manner, a Spirit-filled believer can quickly relate to another Spirit-filled believer within moments of meeting one another. Just as the flesh-man is attracted to the desires of the flesh, so is the spirit-man attracted to the things of the Spirit, but the opposite is also true, for the flesh simply cannot relate to the Spirit. It's a universal law. (1 Corinthians 2:10-16)

Another element pertaining to the law of attraction is: those things that you focus on, you become like. If you spend your time focused on reality television shows dramatizing the dysfunctional behavior of families, don't be surprised when your own family gets nominated for the "Jerry Springer Show." Or if you are hooked on fight to the finish, no holds bar, cage wrestling championships, don't be surprised when everyone around you keeps alluding to what an aggressive, short-tempered jerk you have become. But even with that said, you still need to live according to your own convictions and work out your own salvation with fear and trembling. (Philippians 2:12)

What You Focus On
Focused attention comes not only though what you dwell or think on, but also through the eye gate, the ear gate, and any other gate you might leave open.

"And when He had come out of the boat, immediately there met Him out of the tombs a man with an unclean spirit, who had his dwelling among the tombs; and no one could bind him, not even with chains, because he had often been bound with shackles and chains. And the chains had been pulled apart by him, and the shackles broken in pieces; neither could anyone tame him. And always, night and day, he was in the mountains and in the tombs, crying out and cutting himself with stones."
-Mark 5:2-5

Do you suppose that dwelling among dead men's tombs had anything to do with the man who had the unclean spirit? If you spent day and night surrounded by those who are dead to the things of God, do you think it would affect your life in the spirit? Yes, it certainly would! Be careful whom and what you surround yourself and your business with.

"Watch and pray, lest you enter into temptation. The spirit indeed is willing, but the flesh is weak." -Matthew 26:41

The Law Of Increase

The law of increase directly relates to the principle of producing after ones own kind. For a good tree does not bear bad fruit, nor does a bad tree bear good fruit. For every tree is known by it's own fruit. For men do not gather figs from thorns, nor do they gather grapes from a bramble bush (Luke 6:43-44). The type of seed that you sow denotes the type of harvest you will reap. This is more than an undeniable principle; it's a universal law.

When you plant a seed, the ground yields a harvest according to that seed. The ground can only give back to you that which you gave to the ground. When you plant an apple seed, you expect an apple tree to spring forth. You put money in the bank; you expect the bank to return interest. When you smile at others, they smile back at you (Well, most of the time anyway). If you sow worry, doubt, and fear, then by all means, worry, doubt, and fear is what you should expect to reap. This is the universal law of reciprocity. It's the nature of how things produce and reciprocate with one another.

Something For Nothing

Too many people expect something for nothing. They want God to give them something when they themselves have not invested in the kingdom of God even with the slightest of seeds. Christ calls them hypocrites! They draw near to Him with their mouth, and they honor Him with their lips, but their heart is far from Him (Matt 15:7-9). For where your treasure is, there your heart will be also (Matt 6:21). Understand and learn from the natural laws that God has laid out before you. Know what kind of harvest you want in your business, and plant seeds of the same nature. If you desire obedience from your staff, then sow clearly defined directions and instructions. If you want diligence, then sow commitment. If you desire mercy, then sow compassion.

Weed Seeds

You can sow seeds by the thoughts you harbor in your own mind, by the words you speak, and by the actions you do. If you know that your seed will increase and produce after it's own kind, then you may want to stop and think about what kind of seed you are about to sow; whether it is in your mind, out your mouth, or through your actions. Are you about to plant a field of weeds? If so, you're going to have to harvest that same field of weeds. A business full of spiritual weeds is a very unpleasant place to be!

Since the universal law of sowing, attracting, and increasing is unchangeable, it's a wise thing to take it seriously, for there are severe consequences for those who ignore them. The natural law of increase does not judge what you should or should not do, but this inevitable law does reproduce exactly as you sow. So, sow wisely.

Sowing To The Spirit

Seeds sown to the Spirit reap delayed gratification but long term gain. When you sow to the things of the Spirit, then things of the Spirit you shall reap. When you sow in a spirit of love, then love you shall reap. When you sow generosity, then abundance you shall reap. This is God's universal law of divine reciprocity. You give; God gives in return.

"But this I say: He who sows sparingly will also reap sparingly, and he who sows bountifully will also reap bountifully. So let each one give as he purposes in his heart, not grudgingly or of necessity; for God loves a cheerful giver. And God is able to make all grace abound toward you, that you, always having all sufficiency in all things, may have an abundance for every good work. Now may He who supplies seed to the sower, and bread for food, supply and multiply the seed you have sown and increase the fruits of your righteousness." -2 Corinthians 9:6-8 & 10

One of the most recognized parables that Jesus taught is the parable of the sower and the seed...

"Behold, a sower went out to sow. And as he sowed, some seed fell by the wayside; and the birds came and devoured them. Some fell on stony place, where they did not have much earth; and they immediately sprang up because they had no depth of earth. But when the sun was up they were scorched, and because they had no root they withered away. And some fell among thorns and the thorns sprang up and choked them. But others fell on good ground and yielded a crop: some a hundredfold, some sixty, some thirty. He who has ears to hear, let him hear!" -Matthew 13:3-9

"Therefore hear the parable of the sower: When anyone hears the word of the kingdom, and does not understand it, then the wicked one comes and snatches away what was sown in his heart. This is he who received seed by the wayside. But he who received the seed on stony places, this is he who hears the word and immediately receives it with joy; yet he has no root in himself, but endures only for a while. For when tribulation or persecution arises because of the word, immediately he stumbles. Now he who received seed among the thorns is he who hears the word, and the cares of this world and the deceitfulness of riches choke the word, and he becomes unfruitful. But he who received seed on the good ground is he who hears the word and understands it, who indeed bears fruit and produces: some a hundredfold, some sixty, some thirty." -Matthew 13:18-23

When you receive the Word of God with all readiness, good fruit will develop. And it is just that, a developing process. Just as an apple doesn't ripen overnight, neither will your fruit ripen overnight. It's a maturing process, both personally and professionally. In the business arena, prospecting, networking, and advertising work the same way. As long as you sow on good ground, your business will produce a harvest. But be patient and wait for it, for it will surely come.

Seeds Received: What You See...Hear...Speak...Think
There are many avenues for both good seeds and bad seeds to affect you personally and to grow in your business. Let's look at the other side of sowing: receiving. How do you actually receive seeds that are planted in the spiritual realm? Through the eye gate, the ear gate, the mouth gate and the mind gate.

"The lamp of the body is the eye. If therefore your eye is good (healthy), your whole body will be full of light. But if the eye is bad (evil), your whole body will be full of darkness. If therefore the light that is in you is darkness, how great is that darkness." -Matthew 6:22-23

"So then faith comes by hearing, and hearing by the word of God." -Romans 10:17

"Death and life are in the power of the tongue." -Proverbs 18:21

"I beseech you therefore, brethren, by the mercies of God, that you present your bodies a living sacrifice, holy, acceptable to God, which is your reasonable service. And do not be conformed to this world, but be transformed by the renewing of your mind, that you may prove what is that good and acceptable and perfect will of God." -Romans 12:1-2

If death and life truly are in the power of the tongue, then what you speak holds the ability to either proclaim life or produce death. The very words you speak can either set sail to your business or cause it to sink! Take a look at the way James, the brother of our Lord, describes this phenomenon...

"Indeed, we put bits in horses' mouths that they may obey us, and we turn their whole body. Look also at ships: although they are so large and are driven by fierce winds, they are turned by a very small rudder wherever the pilot desires. Even so the tongue is a little member and boasts great things. See how great a forest a little fire kindles! And the tongue is a fire, a world of iniquity. The tongue is so set among our members that it defiles the whole body, and sets on fire the course of nature; and it is set on fire by hell. For every kind of beast and bird, of reptile and creature of the sea, is tamed and has been tamed by mankind. But no man can tame the tongue. It is an unruly evil, full of deadly poison. With it we bless our God and Father, and with it we curse men, who have been made in the similitude of God." -James 3:3-9

Seeds Spoken: The Bridled Tongue

The tongue is such a small member of the body as a whole, yet it holds the same power as the tiniest mustard seed. When you speak life giving Biblical principles in and through your business, by faith, you have the ability to move mountains. And in like manner, when death, doubt and condemnation roll off your tongue, you have the ability to bring destruction upon yourself, your business, and others who are around you. Like James said, no man can tame the tongue, only Christ in you can bring your tongue, your speech, your attitude, and your actions under the submission of God.

"I will instruct you and teach you in the way you should go; I will guide you with My eye. Do not be like the horse or like the mule, which have no understanding, which must be harnessed with bit and bridle, else they will not come near you." -Psalm 32:8-9

The Scriptures compare the unbridled tongue to that of a fool without understanding. Solomon goes on to say, don't even answer a fool according to his folly, lest you become like him (Proverbs 26:4). This is where that old saying, "Bite your tongue" comes into play.

The principle of Seed Time & Harvest is so vast to say the least, but our hopes from the preceding pages are that a foundation has been laid to understand the importance of the nature of a seed. It has such a small beginning, but when cultivated and watered, it has the potential to reap an abundant harvest. Now it's time to bring this subject into more specific details pertaining to the business arena of the faith-based company.

CHAPTER NINE:
A Time To Cultivate

Before you can plant a seed, you need to cultivate the ground. As far as cultivating in your business is concerned, we'll be expanding on the effects of prospecting, networking, and establishing covenants as a part of the faith-based company's cultivation process in this chapter.

Dictionary.com defines "cultivate" as - to break up in preparation for sowing or planting, to try to acquire or develop. It's no secret that breaking up the competition is often a part of preparation for planting a new business with the intent to acquire or develop the favor of prospective clients.

As an entrepreneur, cultivating the land that you intend to sow is different from that of the employee. It takes a greater degree of effort. It comes with greater responsibilities and greater warfare, but it also comes with greater rewards. As an employee, there may have been times when you were spoon fed manna. But, now you will need to cultivate the land in order to eat of its produce.

"And they ate of the produce of the land on the day after the Passover, unleavened bread and parched grain, on the very same day. Then the manna ceased on the day after they had eaten the produce of the land; and the children of Israel no longer had manna, but they ate the food of the land of Canaan that year." -Joshua 5:11-12

Adam's Curse & Noah's Promise
To one a curse, to another a promise; faith is acknowledging the curse while at the same time proclaiming the promise over it! To understand this better, it's the equation of what you get when you add the promise of Noah to the curse of Adam...

"Then to Adam He said, 'Because you have heeded the voice of your wife, and have eaten from the tree of which I commanded you, saying, You shall not eat of it: Cursed is the ground for your sake; In toil you shall eat of it all the days of your life. Both thorns and thistles it shall bring forth for you, and you shall eat the herb of the field. In the sweat of your face you shall eat bread till you return to the ground, for out of it you were taken; for dust you are, and to dust you shall return.'"

"And the Lord smelled a soothing aroma. Then the Lord said in His heart, 'I will never again curse the ground for man's sake, although the imagination of man's heart is evil from his youth; nor will I again destroy every living thing as I have done. While the earth remains, seedtime and harvest, cold and heat, winter and summer, and day and night shall not cease.' "
-Genesis 3:17-19 & 8:21-22

Understand that the curse on mankind is a result of the sin nature in man, but with that curse God has also given a promise. Though sin is still present in man, there still remains an everlasting promise to man despite the sin nature within. Yet man is cursed with death, he still has a promise of eternal life through Christ Jesus. And likewise, though man is cursed to work and cultivate the ground, he still has a promise that his seed will produce a harvest.

Cultivation: A Group Effort
If your business is founded on a one-man show it's possible but certainly not as easy or productive to cultivate your land alone. God's Word is packed full of admonitions that illustrate the precept of how much more two can do together than one can do alone. Prospecting, networking and making covenant relationships all capitalize on this Biblical precept.

Before you form any covenant relationship, it is a must that both parties are walking in one accord, for how can two walk together unless they are agreed (Amos 3:3). Walking together requires a mutual vision or ambition shared by both parties. This mutual understanding should be both Christ-centered and Spirit-filled.

Let's look for a moment at what a Christ-centered land might look like. The book of Ezekiel closes with just such a vision, a vision that depicts what a rightly divided, well-watered, and cultivated land looks like. The Lord shows Ezekiel not only how the land is to be divided upon the return of the Israelites from captivity, but also, of most importance, He shows him the river of living waters that flows throughout the land. Along the banks of this river all kinds of trees grow and yield fruit, and they never wither, nor will their fruit ever fail. But they will bear fruit every month because their water flows from the sanctuary (Ezekiel 47:12).

This is the same living water of God's Word that runs through your business giving life and healing to all who will drink of it. Your response, like Ezekiel, is to simply stand to your feet, hear what the Lord is telling you, see the vision the Lord is showing you, and be obedient to the call on your life to walk by faith, both personally and in your business!

Ezekiel goes on to say in chapter 48 how the allotment of the land is divided in such a way that the temple of God is centered amongst all the tribes of Israel. "And the land that is adjacent to the holy section, it's produce shall be food for the workers of the city, and the workers of the city, from all the tribes of Israel, shall cultivate it." (Ezekiel 48:18-19)

How does this relate to your business? When Christ is at the center of your business, your business becomes like the fertile land of Ezekiel's vision. Regardless of how tough the economy may get, you can stand on the promise that as long as your business remains adjacent to the "holy section," it's produce shall remain and those who work for the establishment shall be fed by the establishment, and all are to take a part in the cultivating process. (To learn more about the vision of the life flowing river, check out to Ezekiel 47:1-12.)

Prospecting Done Right
Prospecting in the business arena is also known as farming; the systematic collection of leads regarded as potential customers. Prospecting for customers is the first step to consummating any sale and it must be a high priority in your business. You can have the best product or service, but if no one knows about it, then no one is going to buy it.

When done right, prospecting will have a significant impact on the success of your business. For starters, it's important to have what is often called an elevator pitch. This will assist you in opening up dialogue with your prospective customers. It will also be your aid when you suddenly have that last minute freeze as your prospective client answers the phone or walks in the door and you completely forget what you were going to say. Don't be fooled to think it could never happen to you! Play it safe, be prepared at all times.

What Is The Purpose Of The Elevator Pitch?
Elevator pitches are developed to relay just enough information to cause your listener to say, "Tell me more." It is the most powerful and concise presentation of you and your company or its products. It articulates the ideals covering all of your most critical aspects and is delivered within a few seconds; the approximate duration of an elevator ride, usually 40 words or less. Most importantly, it must encourage the listener to respond with, "Please, tell me more."

The elevator pitch is not designed to make or close any sale, but to simply draw in the interest of the listener. If your pitch is done right and spoken or presented before the right audience, then if they are interested, they'll be prompted to ask you for more information. If not, then either they are not interested or your pitch needs a little help.

Few people in the sales arena are prepared with an elevator pitch. And even if they are, it's often mediocre at best. Usually this is not to the fault of the salesperson, but is attributed to the fact that no one within the organization, from the owner to the janitor, has ever bothered to take the time to write down and clearly articulate the client's benefits of doing business with their establishment. Many try to get by simply by stating that it's their service that sets them apart, but isn't that what most of the competition says?

Your elevator pitch needs to clearly state who you are and what you do. It should be a reflection of yourself that ultimately "wows" the listener. When writing your elevator pitch, be more concerned with content than creativity. Recently we came across a brief, yet well defined and precise elevator pitch on "You Tube" that went something like this... "Hi, I'm Paul Blart, and I help my clients increase their sales, improve their profit margins and grow their businesses. Can I help you do that? Maybe. Check out the following video if you want to know how..."

It says who he is, what he does, and how you can benefit from a business relationship with his company. It does not go for the sale, but generates the leads of those who are interested. We consider this a job well done. Let's look at a few more examples. Each one is a little different, yet they all belong to the same research company, Trek Research...

"For restaurants that need to measure and improve customer satisfaction, Trek Research provides the answers you need in half the time through its proprietary combination of online and offline survey techniques." (31 words)

"If you're a restaurateur and can't keep your regulars coming back, you're lost. Using proprietary online and offline survey techniques, Trek Research will find out how you can stop the losses and start generating profit." (35 words)

"Trek Research helps restaurants improve customer satisfaction so that people keep coming back. Nobody else does it the way Trek Research does it — with a combination of both telephone and Internet contacts." (32 words)

If you operated a restaurant that is having trouble discovering why your business is not retaining its customers, or why your advertising dollars are not paying off, then the elevator pitch of Trek Research might have peeked your curiosity to find out more. In that case, mission accomplished.

Writing An Elevator Pitch

This involves three important elements: developing, memorizing, and adjusting a few simple yet incredibly powerful words.

1. **Design And Develop:** Who are you? What do you do? What is your niche market? What differentiates you from others? What is the key benefit to the client? In a nutshell: answer these questions clearly and precisely in such a way that it leaves your prospective listener wanting to know more.

2. **Memorize And Iterate:** It seems simple, but the hard part is keeping it to just 40 words. Continue editing, rehearsing and practicing until it becomes routine but not mundane. Make sure your deliverance is crystal clear and your audience understands the message you're trying to get across.

3. **Adjust And Tweak:** You may encounter different audiences within the same target niche, so make sure your terminology and acronyms fit your specific audience members. Keep your elevator pitch at the appropriate level of your listening audience, not above them and not beneath them.

Christ's Elevator Pitch
Let's look at one more example, this time from the Scriptures. Consider this, if you will, one of the many elevator pitches of Christ...

"I am the way, the truth, and the life. No one comes to the Father except through Me. I am the vine, you are the branches. He who abides in Me, and I in him, bears much fruit; for without Me you can do nothing." -John 14:6 & 15:5

In these two verses, Christ states who He is, what His purpose is, how you can benefit from doing "business" (having a relationship) with Him and the consequences of not doing so. With a few distinct and deliberate words (45 in NKJV to be precise), His elevator pitch hits all the necessary bullet points and leaves the listener wanting to know more. A fantastic example to emulate!

Get Others Involved
Elevator pitches that represent a company or a product must be used by all employees in the company, including the sales team and the executive team. Each of these groups can help hone the elevator pitch. They may even be able to provide alternate versions that they have tailored for their typical audiences. Soliciting their input and feedback on these critical 40 words can help take your elevator pitch up to the next level.

Don't forget that the goal of a successful elevator pitch is to prompt your recipient to ask you the all-important request, "Please, tell me more."

Engaging With Your Client
Now that you've gotten the attention of your prospect, they've heard your elevator pitch, and they have asked you that oh-so-sought-out request of, "Please, tell me more," it's time to interact with your new lead to see if they qualify as a potential client.

It is important to know who your prospects are. In order to provide information that is relative, you need to know a little about who your listening audience is, what their likes and dislikes are, and what their needs are as they pertain to your business. If you were a manufacturer of children's specialty sportswear, then it would be in your best interest to know what sport your prospect is involved in and whether they're shopping for a boy or girl. It certainly doesn't make sense to elaborate on how great your boys rugby gear is, when your prospect is a female tennis player.

Ask Deliberate Questions
When engaging with your prospect, it is important to have a list of questions handy, not only to get their interest, but to better qualify them as a potential customer. These questions can also aid in setting up appointments, if that applies to the nature of your specific business. Use open-ended questions that elicit a response other than yes or no. Always try to close or wrap these questions around an action. For example:

Children's Specialty Sportswear & Outfitters:
"Tell me, what type of sports does your child enjoy playing? Boy or girl?" Tennis: "How has your child's current racket been working out for her?" "Has your daughter mentioned anything about sore wrists or forearms? The wrong weight or size of racket can sometimes do more harm than good if they're not fitted properly to your child's size and abilities. Would you like to see the best options for your daughter specifically?" "What are your daughter's favorite colors? Team colors?" "Are you more concerned with price or performance options?"

These types of questions allow the salesperson to better cater his presentation to the wants and needs of the client. Consider the apostle Paul, he adjusted his presentation depending on who he was speaking with. To the Greeks, he related to their intellect, but to the Jews, their traditions.

Qualifying prospects or selling to customers is never about you, but rather, it must always be about the client! To think otherwise, only leads to a foolish and selfish demise. It's like a slow fade to a sudden death. In the same manner, when God sent His Son to this earth, everything that He did was so that we could relate to Him, not Him to us.

Take time to make a list of questions that will assist you in better presenting your business, service, or products to others. Keep in mind; sometimes, evasive questions are much less threatening or offensive than a direct approach.

For example, if your were working with a prospect regarding financing, rather than asking him if he has a mortgage on his house, you might say, "Which institute or bank is your home financed through?" How you serve something up can make a big difference in the type of response you get. Speak to your client the same way you would like to be spoken to. Ask questions in a way that is non-threatening to answer. The same things that annoy you probably annoy your prospects as well. Be sensitive to this as you develop your list of questions.

Networking With Others

According to Business Dictionary.com, networking is defined as: Creating a group of acquaintances and associates and keeping it active through regular communication for mutual benefit. Networking is based on the question, "How can I help?" rather than, "What can I get?"

For all practical purposes the above definition fits the point we want to establish quite well. Another term used for networking is "Fusion Marketing." Either way you phrase it; it is the concept of forming strategic alliances with similar businesses of a non-competing nature. Entrepreneurs often think they have to go it alone, but it's amazing to see the synergy available from aligning or collaborating with others of a like-minded nature.

Fusion Marketing

In fusion marketing a collaborator is a business that has a similar target market as you but doesn't necessarily compete with your business. Some examples of this would be a graphic designer and a printer, a real estate agent and a mortgage broker, a wedding photographer and a caterer. According to the marketing industry you could collaborate with just about any business out there with limitless possibilities. However we, on the other hand, encourage you to use caution and wise discretion when forming business alliances.

The Scriptures provide many examples of profitable alliances, such as Hiram King of Tyre and King Solomon; King David & Jonathan; Moses and Aaron; the apostle Paul and Barnabas, and many others. But the Scriptures also warn us not to be unequally yoked with unbelievers. King Asa's alliance with Syria resulted in many ongoing wars. Solomon's multiple marriage alliances with other nations led to the onslaught of great idolatry throughout Israel and ultimately the turning away of his heart from God. Samson's alliance to Delilah and the Philistines led to betrayal and grave consequences. When King Hezekiah allowed Babylon (his enemy with whom he was at peace) to see all his treasures, it resulted in the loss of all those treasures.

The bottom-line to networking and fusion marketing is that it can prove to be a tremendous asset to your company when aligned properly. There are multiple factors to consider when collaborating with others, but the greatest of these is that you are of like mind with the same ultimate agenda and vision for the success of your businesses. Know whom you are doing business with and how that relationship aligns with the Scriptures. Do your research.

Are you ready to create a strategic alliance with a similar business and watch both your business grow...

A person walks into the dry cleaners to drop off his shirts and finds a $5 off coupon for the pizza place two doors down. He decides it's time for lunch and pizza sounds good, so he walks down to the pizza place. As he redeems his coupon, he finds a $5 off coupon on the counter for the dry cleaners he was just at. These two establishments are sending traffic to each other. They have formed a strategic business alliance, otherwise known as fusion marketing.

Fusion marketing can be achieved in a variety of different ways in addition to the coupon example above. You can join each of your mailing lists together to produce a joint mailer, cutting down on printing and mailing expenses. Or you can offer an incentive program from purchases referred by your alliance partner and vise-versa. It's a win-win situation when you can work in a spirit of cooperation rather than competition.

To get started, you need a straight set of deliberate, planned out steps, with a reasonable degree of communication and execution.

Setting Up Your Fusion Marketing Arrangements
These steps are relatively simple. We have outlined a few of the basic steps needed to get you started in the right direction.

Step 1: Align With Your Partners: Your fusion partner is someone who has similar prospects as you and could benefit from the same type of prospects that you have, yet their business is not of a competing nature. Examples: builder/landscaper, realtor/mortgage broker, massage therapist/ chiropractor.

Step 2: Define Your Offers: Discuss with your partner what each party will offer. Maybe the wedding photographer provides two free 8x10's while the florist takes 20% off the bridal bouquet. Maybe the chiropractor offers a free exam and X-ray while the masseuse offers a free 15-minute chair massage to first time clients. Figure out what joint offers make the most sense.

Step 3: Confirm Your Agreement: Put in writing who will be doing what. Lack of communication can be your biggest hindrance if ignored. This need not be a major-league document but a clearly drawn up email can suffice. Be creative and be benefit oriented. What's in it for the prospect? As we stated earlier, before forming any long-term or binding alliance, make sure both businesses are operating in one accord with like-mindedness.

Step 4: Combine Your Contacts: Combine your mailing lists and communicate to both lists. Don't worry about who has more or less just combine them. When you put your list with their list you both have a much bigger list than if you did it alone. This can be done with direct mail, e-mail, or both, e-mail certainly being the less costly route.

Step 5: Respond To Responses: Fulfill offers; make it easy to sign up, to buy, to take the next step, and keep track of your shared business. Follow-up and attention will convert prospects into paying customers. Share your leads and your conversions with your fusion partner, as it will be more encouraging to one another. (Proverbs 27:17)

Sometimes you may not know up front whom you want to "fuse" your business with. That brings us to the idea of prospecting for networking partners. You can start by contacting referrals you may get from others you know, or you can obtain a list of a particular nature of business that you might like to join forces with. A good example might be a specialized tile and stone restoration company joining forces with an existing maintenance or janitorial company.

Networking Letters
First communication step: an enticing letter by either direct mail or e-mail to get their attention. Begin by introducing yourself and what your specialty is. Explain the potential benefits to the prospective partner first, followed by the benefits to the prospective clients. Close with your contact information. Keep your letter simple, direct, enticing, and be sure to use easy to read fonts. Make sure your message is clearly understood and highlight the key points you don't want your reader to miss.

Covenant Vs. Commitment

God's Word makes a clear distinction between the two. The word covenant occurs 313 times in the NKJV Bible. The word commitment or its translated counterpart, agreement occurs only 12 times. By His repetition, God seems to be more concerned with the nature of a covenant than a commitment.

The Scriptures refer to a commitment as an agreement or obligation or a vow with a purpose. In the book of Numbers, Moses speaks of the responsibility of a woman who makes a commitment or vow. In a nutshell he states, do what you say you will do, unless your father or husband disagree and cause your vow to become void. A commitment doesn't hold the same weight as a covenant, though both are said to be honored.

So, Why Do We Bring This Up Now?

For the sole purpose of getting you to stop and think about who and what kind of commitment are you making with others in the business arena. When you go to a restaurant, you make a commitment to purchase the meal that you just ordered. Do you have to be of like-mind and share the same goals in life in order to complete the transaction? Of course not.

A covenant, however, is a weightier agreement with greater responsibilities. They are not to be entered into lightly. A covenant with the wrong partner can be a real blessing blocker. They will leverage against your beliefs, rob your resources, and steal your time. Play out all the scenarios before you sign any contact and always make sure you have a way out! Since the majority usually rules according to the world's standards, make sure you hold at least 51% interest, unless you want to be the one getting ruled over. Covenants can cover virtually anything and can be both positive and negative, so be certain you do your research!

Biblical Covenants

People are making them, keeping them, or violating them. All of which we see happening in the Scriptures. Here's a look at what God's Word has to say about Biblical covenants.

They are cut, made and established: usually by God. They are accompanied by a sign. They are accompanied by shed blood. They are everlasting and perpetual. They are confirmed. They are to be kept and held fast to. They are remembered by God. They are not to be forgotten by man. They are not to be made with unbelievers. They are to be obeyed. There are consequences for breaking them. They are not to be forsaken, rejected or transgressed. They are to be respected and are considered holy. They can be executed with vengeance. They can be corrupted and profaned by man. They can contain a curse. They can contain a blessing. They can be made new. They can be made better.

"I have made a covenant with My chosen, I have sworn to my servant David." -Psalm 89:3

"And you shall remember the Lord your God, for it is He who gives you power to get wealth, that He may establish His covenant which He swore to your fathers, as it is this day." -Deuteronomy 8:18

"Behold, the days are coming, says the Lord, when I will make a new covenant with the house of Israel and with the house of Judah, not according to the covenant that I made with their fathers in the day that I took them by the hand to lead them out of the land of Egypt, My covenant which they broke, though I was a husband to them, says the Lord. But this is the covenant that I will make with the house of Israel after those days, says the Lord: I will put My law in their minds, and write it on their hearts; and I will be their God, and they shall be My people." -Jeremiah 33:31-33

CHAPTER TEN:
A Time To Plant

You've selected your seeds and you've cultivated your ground, now it's time to plant those seeds and watch them grow. As far as business is concerned, this chapter of the Seed Time & Harvest section will revolve around advertising and marketing. Advertising is the process of spreading your seeds and marketing is the process of monitoring their growth. Both of which play a huge role in the success of your growing business.

Traditionally, advertising is considered an investment not an expense; with it's marketing purpose being the ongoing process of moving people closer to making a decision to purchase your products or services. We will be exploring these topics, as well as identifying whether your advertising dollars are falling on fertile soil or poor ground, and as usual much more. So now then, let the planting begin!

"Paul planted, Apollos watered, but God gave the increase. So then neither he who plants is anything, nor he who waters, but God who gives the increase. Now he who plants and he who waters are one, and each one will receive his own reward according to his own labor." -1 Corinthians 3:6-8

Advertising: Monitor & Measure

Advertising is often one of the largest budgeted items in a business' financial plan today. Is it really worth it? In order to accurately answer that question, you must have a system in place that monitors the results of your advertising. Do you realize that you can literally double your profits by measuring the results of your advertising campaigns? Some ads will hit the bulls-eye. Others may completely miss the target. Unless you measure, you won't know which is which.

Make it a point to ask each prospect how they heard about you. This doesn't need to be the first question out of your mouth, but it should come up at some point in your dialog with your prospective client. Also, how many of these prospects are converted into sales. If some ads only generate prospects, but never sales, then something needs to be changed. Again you won't know this, unless you monitor and measure it. Measuring your advertising results doesn't need to be complicated. There are many software systems available that will automatically do it for you. If a software program does not cater to the nature of your business, you may want to use a simple tally sheet.

Advertising Workhorses: Commitment & Patience!
Successful advertising requires commitment! A mediocre marketing program with commitment will always prove more profitable than a brilliant marketing program without commitment. Commitment involves not only an investment of financial resources, but also of your time, energy, imagination, and knowledge. Commitment will make things happen.

Patience is the companion workhorse to commitment. When running any advertising and marketing campaign, if you don't have patience, it will be difficult to practice commitment. Patience doesn't mean to continue to run unprofitable, dead-end ads over and over again, patiently waiting for a different result. This is what Webster's defines as insanity. Patience is the capacity to tolerate delays without loosing your peace or getting upset. Remember God's timing is not our timing, nor are His ways our ways (Isaiah 55:8-9). Be committed to the cause and keep standing on God's promises for your life and for your business. Rest assured what He said He will do, He will do!

Practice Makes Perfect
As a new business, it's important to begin your advertising attack in a systematic way. This will help you identify the more profitable targets in your niche market. Each week focus on a set target or group of targets to center your personal advertising and marketing efforts toward. As you stay diligent with one specific target, you will find your pitch and your approach getting better and better. The more you practice and speak it out, the more refined you'll find yourself becoming. On Monday you might sound a little rusty, but don't give up early, by Friday you should be as smooth as silk.

When Joshua led the Israelites into Canaan to conquer the land God had promised them, he did it "little by little." This attack plan was not a form of procrastination, but a deliberate plan set forth by God forty years prior to them even setting their foot in the Promised Land. "Little by little I will drive them out from before you, until you have increased, and you inherit the land." (Exodus 23:30) Their entrance may have been delayed, but when it was time, their attack plan was not: First Jericho, then Ai, then Jerusalem and its surrounding cities, then on to the remaining Southern territory, and then finally the Northern territory. City by city and little by little they conquered their promised land.

The faith-based company has a promised land of its own to conquer. Let's start by looking at a sample attack plan for a local tile and stone cleaning and restoration company.

Week 1:   People I Know & Places I Routinely Go
Week 2:   My Church & Other Local Churches
Week 3:   Schools & Day Care Facilities
Week 4:   Auto Dealerships
Week 5:   Restaurants
Week 6:   Veterinary Clinics & Pest Control Companies
Week 7:   Property Management & Realtors
Week 8:   Hospitals & Urgent Care Clinics
Week 9:   Retirement Facilities & Hospice In-Home Care
Week 10:   Gyms & Health Clubs
Week 11:   Builders & Contractors
Week 12:   Hotels, Resorts & Time Share Facilities
Week 13:   Strip Malls & Shopping Centers

What you plan in the first quarter of a new business will have a huge impact on the weeks, months, and quarters to follow. Take time to write out an attack plan for your company. Pick a target group and stay with that group throughout the entire week. By the time you complete your target list, it should be time to start back at the beginning again.

Of equal importance to where you attack with your advertising campaign is the method of how you attack it. The advertising method that you use matters as much as the actual message that you deliver.

The Method And The Message
The method that you use to market and communicate your specific message has a direct impact on the results you receive. For example, if a nutritional shop were to use a dynamic ad in a well-circulated home

improvement magazine as its advertising method, they'd be better off hitch-hiking on a dead-end road than expecting a big return. A better choice might be a fitness publication or an alliance with a local gym, even if the exposure was before a smaller audience, the expected results would be greater. It is the subtlest failures that kill most advertising campaigns before they ever get a chance to live. It's important to make smart choices for the method as well as the message for your business.

Sales Strategy And Advertising Plans

How and where do you plan to generate new business... through print advertising, media advertising, technology-based advertising, social media, word of mouth?

Within each of these avenues, there will be different vehicles to choose from. Take your time and do your research. Is the message about your business reaching the audience that you want to receive it? An audio clip might reach thousands in a metropolitan gentleman's club, but if you were trying to promote a Christian fitness center that was free of the meat market atmosphere, are you sure that is really the method you want to use to reach your target audience? Just like God's Word, the method and the message are both considered sacred!

In today's society, most advertising is done through common media sources. Media is considered the primary means of mass communication. Among the most common of major media is: television, radio, newspaper, internet, cinema, magazines, billboards, video games, pod casting, and direct mail.

While advertising can be seen as necessary for economic growth, it is not without social costs. It is estimated that consumers encounter between 3500 to 5000 marketing messages per day verses 500 to 2000 in the 1970's. (Consumer & Marketing Watcher) With all this constant media stimulation it is no wonder many people actively avoid commercials today.

We bring this up not to disappoint or intimidate you as a new business owner, but simply to make you aware of what is going on in the advertising arena today. If you want your advertising campaign to stand out, you may need to think outside of the box! A 30-second TV spot can be productive, but it probably won't produce the same kind of results it did twenty years ago, or even ten years ago.

Internet Exposure & Advertising

Since the boom of the Internet started, companies have found new and exciting ways to get the word out about their products and services. Video is a great way to educate prospects about your business and your products or services. YouTube.com and Vimeo.com being the two most popular sources for free video uploading and streaming. However, if it is free, it will be branded.

You can also add video directly to your website for added interest, especially as a welcome or introductory message on your home page. Videos should air like TV commercials, short, direct, and to the point. They should range from 30 seconds to a couple of minutes. Any more than three minutes for any given segment and you will loose their attention.

Some business types reap great responses from audio clips, while others do better from video clips, and still others yet from print advertising alone. If you're not sure what is best for the nature of your business, always test small first, evaluate your results, then move forward!

Audio advertising will vary in lengths, but most radio clips are commonly 15-30 seconds long. Don't worry if you don't feel you have the right voice for audio entertainment. Moses felt the same way, so God sent Aaron to be his mouthpiece. There are a variety of voice-over companies that can provide just the right pitch, tone, attitude, and even accent that you may want to portray your company's message.

Using your elevator pitch for inspiration, you may want to expand on what you already have to develop a few short scripts for an audio advertising campaign.

Website Essentials

A Website is designed to educate your prospects, sell products, or gather lead information. Having a dynamic website doesn't require you to break the bank. In fact, starting with something well done that is both simple and basic will do just fine. The most important basic elements include your Home Page (Serves as your introduction), About Page (Serves to build confidence and credibility), Product Page (Expands on benefits you offer the client), and Contact Page (How the client interacts with you).

Some other essential elements to incorporate into your website include: Get their attention, use meaningful and exciting content, make it well-organized and easy to read, keep them clicking verses scrolling, include helpful links to external sites, highlight graphics that load quickly, be interactive, keep it fresh, updated and real to who you are.

Print Media: It's Time To Start Spreading The News!
Get the word out; put your business in print. Print media is one of the oldest forms of marketing, and it continues to work well for getting exposure if you are a brand new business. Print Media includes (but is not limited to) newspapers, magazines, tri-fold brochures, door hangers, post cards, flyers, CD/DVD envelopes, billboards, and, of course, business cards. It is basically any form of printed marketing material that touches your potential customer.

Ads may come in all shapes and sizes but they all have the same common goal in mind... to expose, entice, and sell a product, a service, or a brand. Text or visuals, or a combination of the two, are the main elements of any print ad. Some print media may have additional special elements such as a business reply envelope, a tear off coupon, a tip sheet or a product sample. It's often the little extras that make a big difference. Try doing something a little special in your business advertising.

Marketing: Business Cards
The infamous business card is an entrepreneur's best friend and his most valuable marketing tool. It is an essential element to becoming unforgettable. Unfortunately, too many people have business cards that simply blend into the mundane multitude only to end up in someone's trash bin. It's a shame, because business cards can be a marketing powerhouse.

Business cards help create a rapport with prospective clients. You find them tucked inside of presentation folders, placed in letters, filed in rolodexes, and used in a myriad of other ways to let people know who you are and what you do. To go from unacceptable to unforgettable, you must...

1. **Evaluate:** How does your card stack up to the rest? If it were mixed in a pile with 50 other cards, are there any features that would cause it stand out?

2. **Create:** Be creative, yet keep it simple. Make sure it's professional, easy to read, informative, and action or benefit oriented.

3. **Initiate:** Print 'em up and hand 'em out! Be excited to share the most amazing marketing tool you have with others! This is no ordinary piece of paper.

So what makes a business card stand out? Research says: a picture or photo that utilizes 1/4 of the card, a black background, an accent of red, and some type of useful chart, table or how-to tip on the backside. These answers might not fit your wants or needs, but you can still apply the ideas in one way or another. How about the chart idea... if you work in an industry dealing with food, or kitchens or homes, include one of your favorite recipes on the back. A photo of you, your business, or an element of what you do will help clients remember who you are. You might also consider adding your logo, one-line slogan, banner Scripture, or another memorable quote.

Direct Response Marketing
Marketing that goes beyond just informing and actually elicits and demands some type of response is known as Direct Response Marketing or DRM. Its ultimate goal is to demand an action!

Too many uninformed businesses waste time and money on advertising that elicits no response. Providing information and exposure can be beneficial, but if it never generates the exchange of a sale, there will soon be serious financial setbacks. Well-done marketing campaigns should arouse the interest of the potential customers to take some type of response to what they have just seen or heard.

The main characteristic that distinguishes a DRM ad from other types of marketing is its driving force of a specific call-to-action. If the advertisement asks the prospect to take a specific action; for instance, making a phone call, visiting a website, filling out a web form, enrolling in a newsletter, or coming into a store location, then the effort is considered to be direct response. Typical Direct Response Marketing channels can include: Direct Mail, Email Marketing, Voicemail or Auto-Text Marketing, Door-To-Door, or Couponing to name a few.

When putting together a Direct Response Marketing campaign consider which channel will generate the biggest response for your specific business. What works for one product or service might not work for the next, so test wisely. Which channels will you use? Take a minute to write down the top five channels you plan to start with.

Call To Action: DRM In The Scriptures

God's Word is packed full of examples of different verses that demand a specific response or elicit a call to action. Among the most obvious are those that pertain to the life of faith. God's very own ad campaign boasts about an eternal life with Him. But in that campaign, God says you must respond by faithing on Him, that is to act upon the belief, sustained by confidence, that God's Word is sure and true and forever settled in heaven. Hebrews 11:6 puts it like this, "But without faith it is impossible to please God, for he who comes to God must believe that He is, and He is a rewarder of those who diligently seek Him."

Let's say, for example, you were feeling weary and tired and needed rest. Where could you go to find that perfect rest? Well, like everything else, God has an ad campaign for just such a need. But you see, in God's ad, in order to find rest, you must do something. There is a specific call to action required. Take a look at God's DRM ad for yourself...

"Come to Me, all you who labor and are heavy laden, and I will give you rest. Take My yoke upon you and learn from Me, for I am gentle and lowly in heart, and you will find rest for your souls. For My yoke is easy and My burden is light." -Matthew 11:28-30

Faith demands a response! If you're looking for rest for your soul, then you might want to respond to this ad.

What about the man or woman who is worn out from trying to attain righteousness by his or her own good works; God says there is a righteousness apart from the law. There is a freedom attained not through good works, but through faith. This faith is near you, it's even in your mouth and in your heart. So, how do you receive what's promised in this ad? "If you confess with your mouth that Jesus is Lord and believe in your heart that God raised Him from the dead, you will be saved." (Romans 10:3-11) The so-called marketing of God's Word demands a direct response. From Genesis to Revelation, It truly is your resource for DRM at its best.

Marketing Mix: Selling vs. Marketing

Selling primarily concerns itself with the tricks and techniques of getting people to exchange their cash for your product or service. Marketing is about the value of the exchange. Proper marketing concerns itself with the entire process; each tightly integrated effort to discover, create, arouse, and satisfy the needs of the customer while generating profits for the company.

The goal of your company's marketing mix is to:

1. **Attract Qualified Leads:** Do the leads being generated have an interest in your product or services? Profitable leads are quality leads, not quantity leads.

2. **Convert Those Leads Into Profitable Sales:** If the leads from any particular marketing channel rarely convert into a sale, then it's probably not a profitable channel, regardless of the quantity of leads.

3. **Retain The Clients You Create In The Process:** Getting the client is only part one, retaining them requires diligence, trust and commitment. Always acknowledge your client's value to you.

Successful marketing campaigns typically require more than one single method of marketing. A business with a good marketing mix will spread its advertising dollars throughout 5 to 15 different marketing channels, each campaign differing in investment cost as well as lead generations produced. The key point is to spread your advertising dollars around in the most profitable mix for your specific business type. It Sounds a little like the Gospel... many different people spreading the message to many different places, in hopes that one might hear and respond!

So, you may be asking, "What is the right marketing mix for your company? Or, "How do you know what to mix? What marketing combinations will work best together? How many different campaigns should you include?" The short answer to such questions is... Research, research, and research!

What's The Competition Doing?
For starters, find out what your competition is doing; not struggling competitors, but those who are making a dent in the market place. Check out their websites and seek out any ads in your market place, which they might be running. It is helpful to find out where they are investing their advertising dollars.

Go online to Google, Yahoo, or your favorite search directories and type in keywords that coincide with your product or service. This is a great way to identify who your competition is.

Don't Be Shy: Get Input And Feedback

Do a focus group (Q & A Feedback) with your current customers or, if your business is new, ask your friends and family to participate. Find out where they would look or go to find you. Take this information and write down the mix of marketing channels they indicated. Rank them by priority, then investment. Then, depending on your advertising budget, identify at least three to five different venues that you will include in your marketing combinations.

You might consider putting 50% of your advertising budget in your best producing market, 35% in the runner-up markets, 10% in other investments and the remaining 5% in experimental campaigns. Make sure that all your marketing combinations complement each other, and take advantage of cross-over advertising whenever you can. Running a TV spot and a radio spot simultaneously would be a good example of a complimenting combination. An example of cross-over advertising would be if you placed a print ad with a local newspaper and then also received exposure in the paper's online publication; it's like double-dipping in a good way.

Fertile Soil Or Poor Ground

How do you determine if the seeds you are sowing (your ads) are falling on poor ground and when is it time to uproot and move your marketing campaign elsewhere? How many times should you run an ad before you give up on it? According to the traditional marketing world, the rule of thumb is run any given ad three times before you halt efforts on it. Well, according to God's Word, He puts a little spin on that number. To see what is meant by that, let's take a look at the parable of the "Barren Fig Tree" in Luke, Chapter 13, for some more insight on the subject.

"He also spoke this parable: 'A certain man had a fig tree planted in his vineyard, and he came seeking fruit on it and found none.' Then he said to the keeper of his vineyard, 'Look, for three years I have come seeking fruit on this fig tree and find none. Cut it down; why does it use up the ground?' But he answered and said to him, 'Sir, let it alone this year also, until I dig around it and fertilize it. And if it bears fruit, well. But if not, after that you can cut it down.' " -Luke 13:6-9

Answer: Give it three good shots, after that fertilize or tweak it a bit, and try it one more time. If still no fruit (profitable leads) come from it, then cut it off. As simple as it is, there is your answer. If your advertising dollars are not producing profitable results after the fourth run, don't get emotionally attached. Cut your losses and move to more fertile ground.

Your ad may have everything right going for it, but if it is airing or running in front of a dead and dry audience, it avails you little. The same principle holds true in the Scriptures. If you haven't received the Gospel message after Matthew, Mark, Luke and John, (four of them by the way) then you're probably not going to get it. Is it because the message (God's ad) was off? Certainly not! The message has simply fallen on deaf and dumb ears, otherwise known as poor ground.

It's important to identify what does not produce a profit! And keep in mind profit isn't always about the sale, but what leads to the sale. Sometimes it takes a few impressions before an exchange will begin to manifest. Be patient and stay committed according to the guidelines and the budget that you set forth.

Setting Appointments
For those who have the concern of setting appointments in their business, here are some tips that will help you accomplish the needed task.

Put the Prospect at Ease: Make sure to state the purpose for your call or visit and the mutual benefit both of you would gain by the meeting.

Take Control: The one asking the questions is the one in control of the conversation. Be bold in asking questions but empathetic with what their plight might be.

Expect The Appointment: More than likely there will be a little resistance before a rapport is established, but the key is to be confident in the benefits you have to offer.

Offer Date And Time Options: Always offer the prospect two dates and times to choose from and avoid using open-ended questions. Try something like... "Will Monday at 2:00 work for you or would Thursday at 4:00 be better?"

Reaffirm After Confirming: Repeat the prospect's entire information back to him accurately. Reaffirming the information helps him to see that he is important to you.

Appointment Incentives: To increase your ability to set appointments consider offering the prospect something in exchange for the appointment. Maybe it's a free demonstration, free quote, or a free gift card.

Bullet Points And Scripts

Depending upon your personal preference, you may want to fully write out what you intend to say to your prospects or you might be more natural at just using a bullet point list of items to cover. Either way, make every phone call conversation as if your client were right in front of you. Pay attention, be enthusiastic, be genuine and stay on point.

When reading the opening scripts of the many epistles written by the apostle Paul, it's interesting to see how they can have a unique comparison to today's phone scripts in the business arena. In Paul's repeated examples, he politely introduces himself with credibility, greets his recipients with genuine sincerity and expresses his thankfulness for them, and then he moves on to the weightier matters. It's a great outline to follow.

Appointment Tips

Setting the appointment is only step one. What you do before, during and after that appointment matters just as much or even more. Here are a few simple tips to keep in mind regarding appointments...

Set Agendas Ahead Of Time: Knowing what you plan to accomplish in a meeting can help maximize your time and aid you in determining how long the appointment should take.

Minimize Travel: Set appointments in close proximity to one another on the same day to maximize your time. Criss-cross travel is time consuming and expensive.

Always Confirm: Reminder calls or emails are a must in almost any industry. Make sure that you confirm the appointment the day before.

Arrive Or Be Ready On Time: Tardiness is among the worst impressions and gestures of unprofessionalism that a business can portray. Consider it one of the seven deadly sins in the business arena! It may be forgiven, but not quickly forgotten.

Send A Thank You Card By The Next Day: As we stated before, it's the little things that make a big difference. Let your prospects and clients know that you value them and the time they spent with you.

Get A Jump On Your Marketing!

You have cultivated the ground and planted the seeds. The topics of Prospecting, Networking, Advertising, Marketing, Attacking, Designing and Mixing have all been covered. Now it is your turn to put it all together into a clearly defined and personalized marketing plan. Your marketing plan needs to map out how you plan to generate leads, where and how much you will invest in your advertising dollars, what you will say, how you will say it, and most of all, what you plan to give away. Keep in mind you don't have to have all the pieces to your marketing plan just perfect in the beginning, that's why it's called a plan. It requires consistent formulating and evaluation to stay in a forward state of motion.

We recommend that you begin with simple, ordinary marketing basics that are put together in an extraordinary and dynamic way. Focus on having these items in place first: Effective business cards, an exciting and informative website, direct response post cards or flyers, social media presence and interaction, a local press release, and fantastic giveaways and incentives.

CHAPTER ELEVEN:
A Time To Harvest

There is a time to plant, a time to cultivate, and a time to bring in the harvest. In the natural sense, harvesting refers to the process of gathering in crops. Figuratively, it refers to the gain of something as the result of an action. If you've taken the appropriate actions to plant and cultivate your business, then now is the time to bring in the gains of your harvest!

Failing to close the sale, work with referrals, maintain repeat clients, or grow your business is like planting a garden that no one ever eats from. Soon, all your crops will just wither away and die. Like many other things in life, harvesting requires diligence. Solomon put it this way, "He who has a slack hand becomes poor, but the hand of the diligent makes rich. He who gathers in the summer is a wise son; He who sleeps in harvest is a son who causes shame" (Proverbs 10:4-5).

"Then He said to His disciples, 'The harvest truly is plentiful, but the laborers are few. Therefore pray the Lord of the harvest to send out laborers into His harvest.' " -Matthew 9:37-38

You have planted, watered and cared for it, and now it's time to "grow" your business by closing the sale. Because each business, product and service is unique, we have decided to include general closing tips that you can personalize to your business.

Close From The Beginning
Don't confuse this idea with the hard sell; the cutthroat approach alienates many potential customers. Instead, explain your agenda. Tell the prospect exactly what you're selling and how it can benefit them. Being up-front

about your intentions promotes an honest, mutually respectful, and rewarding discussion, paving the way for a smooth close.

Learn To Recognize When Prospects Are Ready To Buy
A customer might indicate they are ready by asking questions about the product or the buying process: "How long would delivery take?" "What does that button do?" or "Is an upgrade available?" Other signs include complaints about previous vendors or interested comments such as "Really?" or "Good idea."

Don't Respond To Questions With A Mere "Yes" or "No"
Answer your prospect's queries with questions of your own. If carefully chosen, these return questions can help lead to a sale. For example, instead of answering the question, "Does this come in black?" with merely an affirmative, you could say, "Would you like it in black?"

Free Trials Often Lead Directly To Sales
In sales-speech, this approach is sometimes called the "puppy-dog" close, because it's reminiscent of the attachment children develop to a puppy after keeping it overnight. This strategy works well for all sorts of businesses and appears frequently in magazine subscriptions, where you can receive one month for free. Internet services often use this method by offering free 30-day memberships. And of course there is the auto industry, where potential buyers are offered test drives. The moral of the story: "Try it, you might like it!" And if he likes it, maybe he will buy it from you.

Ask More Than Once
It's almost a habitual, instinctive, natural reaction for you to say, "No" before you even know what you're saying no to. However, more often than not, it's not your final answer. Ask for the sale more than once by isolating the objective and overcoming it nicely and without the garbage of high sales pressure tactics. Remind them of why your business is superior and would be their most beneficial choice. Be patient and consistent and your business will reap a harvest with the right amount of care and commitment.

Referrals
Asking for referrals can have a drastic impact on your bottom-line. If you provide exceptional service that consistently wow's your clients and you ask the right way, you're bound to get referrals most of the time. The

Scriptures clearly state a premise regarding the importance of asking for things; not just anything, but the things that the Father would desire to give us according to His will. We've already established that His will for the faith-based company would include the ability to generate profits and receive blessings, so that you might be a blessing to others. With that premise laid, ask, seek, and knock that the door of referrals might be opened to you (Matthew 7:7-8).

Ask For Referrals

Sometimes referrals will just come to you without your prior knowledge, and sometimes you will need to ask for them. Check out the following sample ideas...

THANK YOU FOR YOUR REFERRAL!

Your business is appreciated, but what we appreciate even more is the impression we made on you. By your referral to a family member, friend or someone you know, we realize we've done our job correctly. To show you this appreciation, we have developed a lucrative incentive program for every referral you send our way.

For every referral you send to (your company name), we will give you 10% of the total bill of their first time cleaning service, no exceptions! We are excited to do this for you. You may use the 10% referral certificate for future cleanings or you can redeem it for cash if you prefer! It's your choice.

It gets even better, we want to offer every referral you send us an enticing 25% off first time cleaning discount. Why are we doing this? It's simple; we want you to know and be reminded that you now have a friend in the business you can trust.

We look forward to doing our best for you and those you know!

NAME, LOGO, CONTACT INFO, SLOGAN, BANNER SCRIPTURE...

We Hope You Are Thrilled With Our Services...
If So, We'd Like To Ask You For A Simple Favor.

Please take a moment to jot down a couple of friends or relatives who would love our work, too. We'll reward you for each referral. When they use our services for the first time, we'll send you $10 in Burns Bucks that you can use as cash toward any service we offer.

CLIENT: _____

1. _____ Phone: _____

2. _____ Phone: _____

3. _____ Phone: _____

NAME, LOGO, CONTACT INFO,
SLOGAN, BANNER SCRIPTURE...

Repeat Business: Invest In Good Ground

Attracting new clients can be costly and time consuming. Investing in your current clients is one of the best investments you can make in your business. Remember, you're creating a culture around your business, not a static standstill. Planting seeds in ground that you already know is good is a great way to maintain and grow your business.

The God Of Repeats

Through and through, the God of this universe is a God of repeat business! For starters, God is in the "feast" business (Leviticus 23). Certainly this seems to be a great repeat business, especially since His people were commanded to keep all the established feasts annually and perpetually in remembrance of Him and what He has done. This included the Feasts of Passover, Unleavened Bread, Firstfruits, Pentecost, Trumpets, Day of Atonement and Tabernacles.

Do This In Remembrance Of Me

Consider the communion table; another repeat business of the Lord's. This, He specifically told you to do often and without limit. Why? In remembrance of Him. Isn't that exactly what business owners want from their clients?

That clients and prospects would continually remember their establishment and repeatedly do business with them! Now then, if you lay the foundation correctly, with the faith-based principles of God's Word, attracted clients will want to continue to be a part of your business.

Cultivate Loyal Clients

Capturing repeat business begins with the mission of cultivating loyal clients who not only keep coming back themselves, but who also tell others through word of mouth marketing. This kind of loyalty requires trust that is developed from multiple contacts and consistently good experiences. Most major businesses nowadays have some type of loyalty program in existence. Consumers' wallets are getting over stuffed with all these loyalty cards. After all, it's easier and more profitable to generate business from repeat clients than to recruit new ones.

To help you create your plan for repeat business with your clients, here are a few simple guidelines and tools you can use...

Never Compete On Price Alone: You must have added value, whether it's a strong guarantee, exceptional service, or a phenomenal product, set yourself apart. Being least expensive in a market generally attracts the price shopper.

Capture Client Information: This is one of the biggest mistakes businesses make when they fail to collect client contact information. If you don't know who your clients are, how will you stay in touch with them? Gather data every opportunity you get.

Hand-Written Thank You Notes: It may seem old fashioned, but it's a great way to show clients that they matter to you. Consider putting something branded with your name or logo in with your note; something that will keep your company in the top of their mind.

Send Out Reminders: It's beneficial to establish a regular system for sending out post card reminders, emails, phone calls or texts; something that reminds your customers that it's time to see you again or come in soon. Including an incentive is good.

Create Your Own Rewards Program: You can offer a discount for having them schedule their next appointment right now, or give a discount or something free after so many purchases.

Conduct Quality Check-Ups: Personally contact the clients within three days after their service letting them know you care about the quality of work performed and their satisfaction. Give them the opportunity to give you feedback. It will make a difference in your business.

Rewards Program Sample Script:
Mrs. Burns, we have a program I think you might like. We call it "Futures." Basically, the way it works is we set your next appointment while we're here with you now. For your scenario, five to six months from today would be ideal. Then, we will call you one week prior to the appointment date to confirm. At that time, you certainly have the option to keep your appointment as is, or you can reschedule for a more convenient time. As long as you keep it within a one to two week period of the originally scheduled appointment, you will receive 10% off your entire bill. We're eager to reward our loyal clients. Sound good?

Giving & Growing
Throughout the introduction of Pillar 2: Seed Time & Harvest, much was said about the principle of seed faith and giving. Not only is it a universal natural law and a good moral principle, it's also the basis for lasting relationships and sound business practices for the faith-based company. The most important bottom-line to this foundational pillar is that in order to grow, you must give!

If you truly believe that you have a product or service that people will fall in love with, then get out there and give it away! For some business owners, this may seem like a tough step, particularly if they view the give-away as lost income or expense drainers. Let us remind you; "God's ways are not our ways, nor are His thoughts our thoughts" (Isaiah 55:8-9). They are unfathomably higher than man's greatest thinking.

Here are a few helpful tips you can use for a successful giveaway...

Have A Superior Product Or Service! Giving away mediocracy is not good enough. It must be better... greater... stronger... faster.

Really Give It Away! Don't go cheap with just a tiny little sample. When Ben & Jerry's Ice Cream opened their doors, they gave away a full sized scoop of ice cream in a cone to every first time costumer that came though their doors. They wanted you to really experience the whole product.

Be Enthusiastic About Giving! Give 'em the whole field. The more excited you are to get your product or service into your clients hands, the more enthusiastic they will be about receiving it.

Treat It As An Opportunity, Not An Expense! Expenses are usually things you owe, but seeds of giving are what you sow.

Give Them A Reason To Come Back! Don't leave it up to chance. Make it worth their while to do business with you. Go Big! Offer a discount for the entire year. Make it easy; no hoops to jump through, no forms to send in; your goal is to get them back. The fewer steps you require of them, the more likely you will be to see them again. Remember to use Direct Response Marketing (DRM) that calls the client into action.

"There is one who scatters, yet increases more; and there is one who withholds more than is right, but it leads to poverty. The generous soul will be made rich, and he who waters will also be watered himself. The people will curse him who withholds grain, but blessing will be on the head of him who sells it." -Proverbs 11:24-26

Scattered Seed equals Increase. Generosity equals Richness. Withholding equals Cursing. Selling equals Blessing. The Scriptures are clear. God loves a cheerful giver (2 Corinthians 9:7). Why? Because they are becoming more like the universe's most generous giver, Christ Himself, and the genuineness of His Spirit in you is proven by the way that you give. The faith-based company is earmarked by its generosity.

The Proverb noted above eloquently shows the seed faith principle taught throughout the David's 400 curriculum. Seeds need to be scattered to gain an increase, in the same way money is to be invested in order to reap more than what is sown. When fear or selfish gain prompts you to hold back more than what is appropriate, the harvest becomes less, not more. Liberal giving is a direct correlation to both spiritual and material prosperity. Consistent giving is equivalent to consistent watering; they both continue to produce a harvest as long as you continue to sow. Giving must be exercised and multiplied in every aspect of your faith-based company!

In the startup stages of any new business venture, the marketing budget is typically limited. Be proactive in your giving by having some promotional ideas on hand that are cost-effective. Here are some different ideas of potential promotions and incentives that can easily be executed...

Free Food: Everybody loves free food. Shop smart and use bulk purchases from warehouse clubs.

Free Consultations Or Demonstrations: If the demo is what sells the job, then by all means do it free and do lots of them.

Free Products To Try: As we said before, if you've got something the public will love then let them try it.

Gift Cards To Local Businesses: Support your community by networking with businesses in your area. Coffee shops, favorite restaurants, and home improvement stores are usually always well received.

Sponsor A Sports Team, School Function, Or Church Event: The more exposure your name gets, the more people will put you first in their mind. What better way to be remembered by then helping out in a way that is personal to your clients?

Contest Winners: Find a prize of interest to your target audience, and hold a contest for them to receive it.

DVD's & CD's: If you have a DVD promoting your company, great; if not, give away one of your personal favorite DVD's or music CD's, preferably ones that might minister to them.

Books & Quick-Study Guides: Our personal favorite, the "Maintenance Manna" by M.L. Moody, a daily study guide through God's entire Word in one year. Available at Davids400.com.

Bibles: This may be the last item on our list, not because of priority, but simply because we saved the best for last. There is absolutely no greater gift on the planet, than God's living and powerful written Word in your hand!

PILLAR 3: PRODUCT KNOWLEDGE

CHAPTER TWELVE:
Pursue Excellence

Congratulations!
You are among the elite group of small business owners who recognize the need for continual growth and improvement in themselves and their businesses. The brutal statistics show that 90% of small business owners will not take any action to improve themselves or their businesses within the next year. It's heartbreaking to see so many businesses failing in today's economy, yet they do nothing to change their situations.

There are many things that play a role in business improvement, one of which is product knowledge with proper application. It will lead to more business and increased sales. It is certainly easier to effectively sell to consumers when you can show how your product, service, or method will meet their specific needs. If you lack knowledge in your own product or service, how will you ever be able to intelligently present it to others?

Regardless of the nature of your business, you must be properly equipped with knowledge of your industry, your product, your equipment, your service, your marketing tools, your prospective clients, your features, your functions, your benefits, and so on, in order to get off to the best start possible. Not only is product knowledge a prerequisite from the onset, but it is also a vital priority for continued success.

Zeal With Knowledge
God's Word tells us that zeal without knowledge is dangerous, and that His people perish for lack of knowledge (Romans 10:2, Hosea 4:6).

Enthusiasm is contagious, but it must be accompanied by knowledge to be properly grounded. The business arena is no exception to this rule! Pillar 3 is geared toward unfolding the relevance of product knowledge from a Biblical perspective.

"Be diligent to present yourself approved to God, a worker who does not need to be ashamed, rightly dividing the Word of Truth." - 2 Timothy 2:15

Pursue Excellence

Operating your business with a spirit of excellence is not the result of operating in perfection, but rather operating with a spirit of diligence. In our banner Scripture for Pillar 3, Paul admonishes Timothy to "be diligent." This Hebrew word refers to exerting oneself, to study, to endeavor. Dictionary.com translates endeavor as, "to try hard to do or achieve something, as in an utmost attempt to achieve a goal."

Knowledge Requires Diligence

Some individuals may seem to be more naturally keen than others, but knowledge doesn't just fall into anyone's lap. It is gained through things taught, through things seen and heard, through things received and through things experienced. Each of these learning gateways requires some form of endeavor. Let's take a look at what the apostle Paul writes about wisdom in his epistle to the church at Ephesus...

"See then that you walk circumspectly, not as fools but as wise, redeeming the time, because the days are evil. Therefore do not be unwise, but understand what the will of the Lord is. And do not be drunk with wine, in which is dissipation; but be filled with the Spirit." - Ephesians 5:15-18

Redeem The Time

Knowledge is gained when you walk circumspectly, or carefully. It is seizing and capitalizing on every appropriate moment set before you. Life is short, or as King David wrote in the Psalms, it is but a vapor. Take advantage of the time God has given you, and use your time wisely. Knowledge can be obtained through study, but wisdom is knowing how to use that knowledge. Take time to allow God to manifest His wisdom in you, through His Word and by His Spirit. Note: True Biblical knowledge points to having an understanding of what God's will and purpose are for your life and how you will ultimately reflect that revelation in your faith-based company.

Back to our banner Scripture in 2 Timothy 2:15... How does a worker avoid being ashamed? He must rightly divide God's Word. This means "to cut things straight" or to teach the truth directly and correctly. Whether it's cleaning tile floors or serving exquisite meals on wheels, you have a truth about your business that you are required to know and understand. How you directly and correctly communicate that truth to your client can make you or break you. Rightly dividing knowledge about your specific industry and applying it through proper wisdom will set you apart from the competition. To rightly divide something means to properly understand it. In chapter three, Paul writes to Timothy,

"But you must continue in the things which you have learned and been assured of, knowing from whom you have learned them, and that from childhood you have known the Holy Scriptures, which are able to make you wise for salvation through faith which is in Christ Jesus. All Scripture is given by inspiration of God, and is profitable for doctrine, for reproof, for correction, for instruction in righteousness, that the man of God may be complete, thoroughly equipped for every good work." -2 Timothy 3:14-17

Wisdom And Correction
When you are assured the information that you are receiving and studying is true, accurate and correct, you are to stay in that doctrine, or body of teaching. If you walk in the confidence that God's Word holds the answers to every question in life, then regardless of your industry, there is a means of confirming what you learn through His Word. The wisdom and correction obtained through the Scriptures is what makes the man or woman of God complete. Rightly dividing and understanding that wisdom and correction is part of the process of being thoroughly equipped.

Resistant And Gullible
Paul also warns Timothy about those who are always learning but never able to come to the knowledge of the truth. They are resistant men of corrupt minds and gullible women loaded down with sins and led away with

various lusts. They will progress no further, for their folly will be manifested to all (2 Timothy 3:1-9).

That has got to make you stop and think which group of learners are you in...

"No prophesy of Scripture is of any private interpretation or origin." - 2 Peter 1:20

CHAPTER THIRTEEN:
Properly Equipped

Operating any business without being properly equipped is not only foolish, it's dangerous. People can get hurt, including you, your staff, and your clients.

King David learned this lesson the hard way. God laid out some clear and precise directions for how He wanted certain things done. This information was available to King David. He just needed to do the proper research to obtain it. In King David's zeal for the Lord, he somehow missed the directions. Was it rebellion or did David simply skip over gathering all the information and knowledge necessary to complete the business at hand? You decide.

"And David arose and went with all the people who were with him from Baale Judah to bring up from there the ark of God, whose name is called by the Name, the Lord of Hosts, who dwells between the cherubim. So they set the ark of God on a new cart, and brought it out of the house of Abinadab, which was on the hill; and Uzzah and Ahio, the sons of Abinadab, drove the new cart. And they brought it out of the house of Abinadab, which was on the hill, accompanying the ark of God; and Ahio went before the ark."

"Then David and all the house of Israel played music before the Lord on all kinds of instruments of fir wood, on harps, on stringed instruments, on tambourines, on sistrums, and on cymbals. And when they came to Nachon's threshing floor, Uzzah put out his hand to the ark of God and took hold of it, for the oxen stumbled."

"Then the anger of the Lord was aroused against Uzzah, and God struck him there for his error; and he died there by the ark of God. And David became angry because of the Lord's outbreak against Uzzah; and he called the name of the place Perez Uzzah to this day."

"David was afraid of the Lord that day; and he said, "How can the ark of the Lord come to me?" So David would not move the ark of the Lord with him into the City of David; but David took it aside into the house of Obed-Edom the Gittite. The ark of the Lord remained in the house of Obed-Edom the Gittite three months. And the Lord blessed Obed-Edom and all his household."

"Now it was told King David, saying, 'The Lord has blessed the house of Obed-Edom and all that belongs to him, because of the ark of God.' So David went and brought up the ark of God from the house of Obed-Edom to the City of David with gladness." - 2 Samuel 6:2-12

Equipped With Instructions

God gave very specific instructions in the book of Exodus how the Ark of the Covenant was to be carried and transported. Had King David gathered and followed those directions, it could have spared Uzzah's life. Three months later, King David tries it again, this time under the specific instructions dictated to Moses.

"Then David said, 'No one may carry the ark of God but the Levites, for the Lord has chosen them to carry the ark of God and to minister before Him forever.' He said to them, 'You are the heads of the fathers' houses of the Levites; sanctify yourselves, you and your brethren, that you may bring up the ark of the Lord God of Israel to the place I have prepared for it. For because you did not do it the first time, the Lord our God broke out against us, because we did not consult Him about the proper order.' So the priests and the Levites sanctified themselves to bring up the ark of the Lord God of Israel. And the children of the Levites bore the ark of God on their shoulders, by its poles, as Moses had commanded according to the word of the Lord.' " - Chronicles 15:2 & 12-15

Each situation we face in life requires us to be properly equipped in order to receive the maximum benefit from that situation. God's lesson: The presence of the Lord is to be carried by people not by things.

Properly Equipped

A business equipped with superior product knowledge should stand out from its competition. Relaying valuable information to your clients in a beneficial way has an illuminating effect, like a lamp that lights up a room. Without it, you just can't see clearly to make the right or best choices. Christ also used this allegory in the gospels.

"You are the light of the world. A city that is set on a hill cannot be hidden. Nor do they light a lamp and put it under a basket, but on a lamp stand, and it gives light to all who are in the house. Let your light so shine before men, that they may see your good works and glorify your Father in heaven." -Matthew 5:14-16

One key thing to note: Don't allow the shining light of your superior knowledge to turn into the dark head of pride, lest God blow out the light when you least expect it. Product knowledge is to be shown with humble confidence and zealous enthusiasm.

As a faith-based company, you are to be the authority over your competition by faith and through properly and continually increasing product knowledge. Know what your competition is doing, but don't be an expert on it. In the same way that Paul admonishes the Christians in Rome to be wise in what is good and simple concerning evil (Romans 16:19), you ought to be diligent in the things of your business and aware, yet not consumed with the things of other or like businesses. God's promises and blessings are priceless to those who are obedient in the faith.

"And the Lord will make you the head and not the tail; you shall be above only and not be beneath, if you heed the commandments of the Lord your God." - Deuteronomy 28:13

Firsthand Knowledge

It's been around for ages. Do you remember the traditional children's game "Telephone?" It is played by gathering a group of people together in a big circle. One person begins by whispering a message to the person beside him. That person then whispers the message to next person, and so on, until the message reaches the last person in the circle. The object of the game is for the last person to be able to accurately state the message given to him. If it matches the original message stated by player one - it's a success! The problem, or as kids might say, the fun part, is that the last person usually never says it correctly. Whether deliberately or incidentally, it's sure to come out scrambled.

Thank God, His Word has been carried through generation after generation and still remains true and infallible. Scribes and translators alike have been martyred over the preservation of God's Word. Unlike the telephone game, great and extensive detail has gone into each stroke of each letter of each word of God's Holy Writ. During the era when the scribes copied the scriptures by hand, the scrutiny process under the Jewish rabbis was intensive. Each and every jot and tittle of every letter was accounted for. If one stroke was missing - out it went!

Get It For Yourself!
Can you imagine what life would be like, it you could only base your belief system on hearsay from other people? How would you ever know if you've got the story straight without going to the original source? Sadly, that is the case for many Christians sitting in the church pews today. They may listen to what the preacher says from the pulpit, but they never get in the Scriptures and berean it out for themselves. What does berean me? See Acts Chapter 17 for details.

Nicolaitan Oppression
Like everything else in life, and as Solomon would say, "There is nothing new under the sun." This behavior is not new, but rather an oppression

that's been passed down for generations. Christ speaks about such an oppression by the Nicolaitans in Revelation 2 verses 6 & 15. In regard to the doctrine of the Nicolaitans, He commends the church at Ephesus for hating the deeds of the Nicolaitans, which I also hate. The meaning of their name gives them away... "Nico," meaning to conquer + "laitan," meaning the lay or common people. Little is mentioned about this sect other than their oppressive conquering spirit over the common people and commentary notations stating, "They lead lives of unrestrained indulgence."

The doctrine of the Nicolaitans is not just something from the past; it is the same spirit that you see today suppressing individuals from learning the Truth for themselves. You can see a form of its manifestation in the workplace when an employee holds back information from his peers in fear of loosing his position. Or it can be seen in a supervisor who provides only the bare minimum information to his staff to function, but not excel, so as to maintain the pride of his authority. Beware that you or your staff are not on either side of this ugly coin.

Receiving information firsthand from a reliable source is one of the best banks of knowledge you can draw on. The only thing above this is firsthand experience. Experiential Knowledge is priceless! If it's product information you need, don't ask your buddy what he did, contact the manufacturer or the local sales rep yourself. If you have technical concerns, go straight to the service department or back-end support. If you need a refund or replacement, contact the warranty division for direct assistance. Policies may vary from situation to situation. Get your answers from the source not the circle.

First Hand Knowledge
"Israel served the Lord all the days of Joshua, and all the days of the elders who outlived Joshua, who had known all the works of the Lord which He had done for Israel." -Joshua 24:31

Second Hand Knowledge
"When all that generation had been gathered to their fathers, another generation arose after them who did not know the Lord nor the work which He had done for Israel." -Judges 2:10

The Result: They forsook God and did evil in his sight. See Judges 2:11-12 for the rest of the scoop.

Features, Functions, Benefits
These things might sound a little cliché, but unless you understand how they relate to one another, you could have a sinking ship on your hands. You may have the coolest gadget with the most awesome features, but if you don't know how it functions, it won't do you much good. Likewise, you might know how something functions, but if there is no direct benefit to you, you're likely not to give it a second thought. Do you see how they fit together and correlate to one another?

The Feature: You, your Product, or your service.

The Function: How you or it works or operates.

The Benefit: How you or it meets the needs, solves a problem or provides a solution for your client.

Whatever the function, you must build features into your product or service, which will enable you to effectively sell its benefits to the end user. If you don't relate your features to your benefits, or if your benefits don't address what's important to your clients, then they probably won't trigger the need to buy. You must know your product or service well enough to identify its direct benefits to those to whom you are marketing.

Let's look at a simple example of this correlation for a carpet cleaning company. Let's say one of the features is an air mover. Its function is to quickly dry carpets. Now you need to relate these features and functions so that the client can directly see the benefit to them...

The Problem: You've got guests coming over for dinner and you can't wait all day for your carpets to dry. The Turbo Clean Solution: We use specialized air moving fans, which will dry your carpet quickly and thoroughly in less than two hours. We realize that even that can seem like a long time when you need it most, so we will also give you a few pairs of plastic booties that you can wear over your shoes. This way you can walk about on your carpet immediately while it is still drying. After all, we're here to help solve your problems, not create them.

God's Features, Functions And Benefits
As with all areas of the David's 400 curriculum, it is our mission to continually align the information contained within each of the pillars to the Word of God as our plumb line. The alignment on this particular principle is a fun one! See for yourself.

Feature: Christ's incarnation
Function: His death and resurrection
Benefit: Our salvation

Feature: Holy Spirit infilling
Function: Guides us into all truth & continually points to Jesus
Benefit: Peace that surpasses all understanding

Feature: Mountain moving faith
Function: Driving force behind our actions sustained by confidence
Benefit: Promises Of God

Feature: God's instructions
Function: Obedience that pleases God
Benefit: Blessings of God

The faith-based company will do well to have at least five to seven of these feature-function-benefit statements about its business well memorized.

Innovate: Always Moving Forward
To innovate means to continuously find new and better ways of doing something, especially by introducing new methods, ideas or products. It doesn't mean you need to reinvent the wheel, but simply continue to make improvements to it. Thankfully, the continual innovation of the wheel itself has brought us out of the Stone Age and into the technology of reinforced, steel-ply rubber tires, resulting in dramatically increased performance and safety.

When you innovate effectively the competition will ultimately copy you and intensify competitiveness. Therefore, as long as competition remains, you will need to innovate again and again. It's a way of life for the forward moving entrepreneur. The positive outreaching effect of innovation is the direct benefit to the consumer. They will continue to receive stronger, faster, better products in the market of almost any industry. Without innovation, we'd still need a hammer and chisel to change our wheels.

The greatest of retailers who stand the test of time, operate with a spirit of innovation. It's main rule of thumb: innovations must be meaningful to the end user! As parents, one of our personal favorites is the innovation of toothpaste your kids will actually like using.

Bubblegum Flavored Toothpaste

It's ingenious! Like many other kids on this planet, our youngest daughter could not stomach the "spicy" flavor, as she would call it, of the traditional adult "minty fresh" toothpaste. Not only has the innovation of kid friendly flavors made an impact on enthusiastic young brushers, but now they can dramatically increase their brushing capabilities with electronic powered toothbrushes of their favorite cartoon friends. What an innovative idea!

Square Patties

Rule #1, make it meaningful. Rule #2, don't be fickle. Don't try so hard to be different that your product or service no longer correlates to your market. Consumers can be very particular about how far outside the box they're willing to go. For example, Wendy's thought outside the bun when they decided to create a square patty for their round bun. Different, yes. Innovative, hmm, maybe. For some consumers, it's simply not sensible enough to appeal to them. A square patty hanging out from a round bun doesn't fit quite right. It seems a little bit awkward, like putting a square peg into a round hole.

Innovations At Work

To really help this hit home, let's look at a few innovations that are currently in the marketplace. We're going to use "The Master's Touch," a faith-based company out of Arizona as our inspirational example of innovations at work.

The owner of this company began his endeavor as an independent carpet and upholstery cleaning company. After a short time in the industry, he began to notice how many job sites had natural stone and tile that needed to be cleaned just as bad as the carpets did. The problem: no tools existed that could use high pressure and hot water to extract and clean these surfaces without damaging them. The solution: innovate a tool that will work! So that is just what he did.

The first tool featured a single-jet wand design, covering a 4" path, capable of cleaning 100-200 square feet per hour. This was a huge innovation for the industry and considered by many the biggest breakthrough in tile and grout cleaning history.

Then it was time to spin the wheels a little harder. What innovative changes in design could help make this tool more productive? Answer: Creating an increase in the surface coverage that would allow for more cleaning in less time. Off to the drawing board it went. Although it was three years in the patenting process, a phenomenal tool was turned out, using dual spinning jets with a high-pressure extraction process now capable of cleaning 1000-1500 square feet in one hour. With this ten-fold improvement in design and profitability has come international recognition as the top performing hard-surface cleaning tool available in the industry today.

It doesn't stop there. The Master's Touch has gone on to produce hand-held versions of both these tools for use on vertical surfaces and hard to reach areas. Both of these have been a huge hit in the marketplace. The original tool has since been updated with quick disconnect features to interchange from a 4" single-jet head to a 16" four-jet head for varied applications and uses. Their latest innovation is a specialized concrete cleaning tool with a 16" cleaning head, which offers more coverage for larger, more expansive areas. One thing to keep in mind from this example is that innovation is always moving forward. It is a dynamic process that never stays stagnant. The innovative spirit sees the need and looks for ways to meet that need or even better, exceed it!

Now, that's innovation at work in the marketplace!

Innovations In The Scriptures: Instruments

Many times the Scriptures say we are to sing to the Lord a new song and shout praises to His name. Ever wondered about the process by which man went from simply singing and clapping his hands to what we now know as a fully embodied orchestra today?

The innovation of the horn is just one of God's many amazing instruments. What began as a simple horn from a ram has now taken on innumerable shapes, sizes, and melodies. When King David prepared to build the Temple, God sent to him many skilled musicians with harps, stringed instruments, and cymbals that had the ability to prophesy through song (1 Chronicles 25:1-8). God hasn't changed the purpose of the instrument, but He has enabled man to improve upon the design and sound quality of it, that we might make a sweet melody unto the Lord.

Innovations In The Scriptures: Weapons

The first weapon ever made for war was a rock tied to a string. David as a young lad learned of its use when he defeated Goliath. Later came the spear, then the javelin, then the bow and arrow. As war became more prevalent in the land, God allowed for innovations that would protect and defend His people.

Even at a time when there were no blacksmiths among Israel, God made a way with innovative weapons such as the weapon of confusion. Joshua led the Israelites with just such a weapon. It was the appearance of lit torches and the sound of numerous clay pots breaking that sent his enemies on the run. God gave King David a similar victory over the Philistines. At the sound of marching in the mulberry trees, God brought confusion and fear over David's enemies and victory to Israel. It seems with God, victory can come through some pretty creative measures.

Innovations In The Scriptures: Earth's Design

Have you ever stopped and considered God's creative design of earth itself? God asked Job such a question. "Where were you when I laid the foundations of the earth? Who determined its measurements? To what were its foundations fastened? Have you comprehended the breadth of the earth? Tell Me, if you know all this." (See Job chapters 38-41). If any one thing were created differently, if the earth was tilted one degree differently, life would not be as you know it!

Innovations In The Scriptures: God's Covenant

Knowing the sinful nature of mankind, God established a covenant with man through the Levitical priesthood and sacrificial system as propitiation for his sins. Each year, atonement was to be made for Israel's sins by the high priest through the sacrifice of a lamb without blemish. Even with this special covenant, God found it necessary to innovate something greater. The Bible tells us that, if the first covenant had been faultless, then no place would have been sought for a second. But, finding fault in the first covenant, God promised a new and better covenant. He will take the stony heart out of your flesh and give you a new heart. He will put His laws in your mind and write them on your heart. He will be your God and you shall be His people. This covenant is made possible only by the shed blood of Christ who has made the final atonement for your sins. Christ came as the High Priest making the final sacrifice for your sins by His perfect shed blood. By such sacrifice you have been redeemed and have a restored relationship with the Father. Without the innovation of this new covenant, there would be no eternal hope of glory for mankind.

Find out more about these covenants in Jeremiah 31:31-34 and Hebrews Chapters 8-10.

Innovative Thinking

Most likely, you can probably think of a number of innovations that persuaded you to change your ways or change your buying patterns. For example the innovation of online streaming has dramatically changed the music industry and its distribution methods. With the current capability to download your favorite song or album right from your home computer, purchasing CD's is becoming a thing of the past for many folks. Or, how about the home video trend sweeping our nation, aka: Netflix. You can now instantly watch movies from your own computer or TV without ever leaving your house. What an innovative idea! It has certainly pushed their competition to reconsider how they will continue to serve their clients.

What have you done recently in your own company that was innovative? Every good and perfect gift comes from above (James 1:17), and that includes the gift of innovative thinking. Take the time to write down your ideas, especially while they are fresh. Likewise, note ideas you might obtain from staff members and consumers. It is an amazing thing what God can do with the smallest or seemingly insignificant idea when it is of Him.

Continual Renewing

In the same manner that reading God's Word one time and then setting it on a shelf to collect dust will stunt your spiritual growth, so will the growth of your business become stunted without continued and furthered education. Many industries have raised their standards over the years through improved technology, better quality equipment, more efficient chemicals, higher levels of training, and so on and so forth. How does your company fit into this improvement process?

Renewal can be found in different ways. It can come in the pursuit of something and it can also come in the process of waiting in faith for something. The prophet Isaiah speaks of a renewing that takes place with those who wait on the Lord. This renewal is a swift motion or quick change, as in substituting something new for something old (Isaiah 43:18-19). Sometimes that's just what a business needs, a swift change in a better direction. Set yourself apart so you can be sensitive to what the Spirit is showing you. Waiting on Him, may hold the renewal you need for yourself and your business.

"But those who wait on the Lord shall renew their strength; they shall mount up with wings like eagles, they shall run and not be weary, they shall walk and not faint." - Isaiah 40:31

Let's look at another example in Psalm 51:10 when King David sought repentance to the Lord after the loss of his first born son with Bathsheba. He cries out, "Create in me a clean heart, O God, and renew a steadfast spirit within me." Renew, in this context, refers to making a repair to oneself (or something) and to restore or polish to a splendor. Steadfast refers to being firmly established, stable, and secure. Spirit, in this context, refers to more than just breathing life. It refers to the moral character or seat of ones mental and emotional acts. When you put this all together, King David is seeking that the Lord would repair and restore the splendor of God's moral character in him in a stable and secure way. This psalm is not exempt to the business arena. Could you imagine if more men and women sought the Lord for this type of renewal in their business? A faith-based company that sought the restored splendor of God's moral character in a firm and established way throughout their company would, no doubt, walk in promises that far exceed the world's idea of a favorable business.

Be Transformed

As the Scriptures show, renewal can come through waiting, through asking, and through pursuing. To those whom God has illuminated, it is a truth that daily Bible reading transforms your thoughts, your minds, your heart, and your soul. Genesis 1 to Revelations 22 is the continual unfolding of who God is and His plan of salvation for His people. Not only that, but to the businessman or woman with illuminated eyes and ears, it is the unfolding story of how to operate a successful business based on Biblical principles. It's all in there, what to do and what not to do, what to emulate and what to turn away from.

Paul writes in his letter to the Romans, that we are not to pattern ourselves according to the world, but we are to completely renew and change our minds (our faculties of perceiving and understanding) for the better good according to God's will. This process takes effort and diligence. It is the process of studying to show yourself approved. It's critical that you never come to the conclusion that you've arrived to your fullest potential of knowledge. For those who think they've arrived, soon will find that they know the least. The more you know, the more you should realize how much you really don't know. Pride always comes before the fall. Are you sure you want to take that trip?

"I beseech you therefore, brethren, by the mercies of God, that you present your bodies a living sacrifice, holy, acceptable to God, which is your reasonable service. And do not be conformed to this world, but be transformed by the renewing of your mind, that you may prove what is that good and acceptable and perfect will of God. For I say, through the grace given to me, to everyone who is among you, not to think of himself more highly than he ought to think, but to think soberly, as God has dealt to each one a measure of faith." -Romans 12:1-3

You must keep your own mind transformed in order to effectively transform others. Find ways to learn more about your industry. Be aware of changing technology. Stay informed about your business, your customers, and your market. Uninformed or misinformed businesses can lead to confusion, which most often, leads to deception. Verify crucial information for yourself firsthand. How does it align with the plumb line of God's Word? If action is required, don't procrastinate. Do it now, while the day is still at hand.

CHAPTER FOURTEEN:
Effective Distribution

It is one thing to have knowledge about your product or service, but it is another thing to correctly communicate that knowledge to others. Having insecurities? Don't worry; you wouldn't be the first to have concerns about your abilities to deliver this task.

Moses felt the same way. He had knowledge of both the ways of the Egyptians and the ways of the Israelites. After Pharaoh's daughter drew Moses out of the river, he was nursed as a child by his own Israelite mother, and went on to be raised in the house of Pharaoh for 40 years. Moses later spent 40 years in the wilderness learning the ways of a shepherd's life as taught to him by his father-in-law, Jethro. He is now at a place in his life where God can use these first-hand experiences according to His will and His greater plan. Moses' response to the call, even after God has shown Himself through miraculous signs...

"O my Lord, I am not eloquent, neither before nor since You have spoken to Your servant; but I am slow of speech and slow of tongue." - Exodus 4:10

God reassures Moses that He is the One who has given him a mouth and He will teach him what to say. Still Moses responds with, "O my Lord, please send by the hand of whomever else You may send." (Verse 13) God resolves to send Moses' brother Aaron to him, to be his mouthpiece. God will still speak directly to Moses and teach him what to say, but Aaron will be the spokesperson to the people.

Discern what your situation calls for. The greatest of many men that God spoke through had concerns of not being the best choice, nor properly equipped for the job. Gideon was from the weakest and smallest of clans. Saul and his family were considered the least of those in Benjamin and the smallest of the tribes of Israel. David was ruddy and the least among his brothers. Jeremiah was only a youth. Isaiah was a man of unclean lips. You too may be the foolish thing that God uses to confound the wise.

If you lack the ability to properly communicate the features, functions, and benefits of your company to others, then ask that the Lord would send you a spokesperson. If the gift isn't there, hire someone who has it! This not only applies to verbal communication, but to print and media advertising as well. It's not an uncommon thing to have voice-overs as part of your video and audio marketing campaigns. If God has called you to do what you are doing, then will you trust Him to run your business His way in spite of whatever inabilities you think you might have?

Pursue Excellence
Spiritual confidence comes through studying God's Word. Natural confidence comes through studying your product or service. If a client is interested, but not fully committed to completing a sale, the difference can sometimes be the lack of confidence a salesperson has in his product. The more educated you become in your product and its uses, the more it will help cement the confidence you need while speaking to others. People want to do business with people who know their stuff.

Role Play
It may take time to get your pitch just right. The more you practice, the better your articulation skills will become. Don't be afraid to role play with others. It is probably one of the best forms of practice you can do. Role play different techniques and methods of presenting your product or service to your clients. This will allow you to become more comfortable with the various types and personality traits you may encounter. Keep note cards handy in case you draw a blank.

King David's Confidence
Remember the story of King David and the Ark? David was hesitant to try anything further after learning his lesson on what not to do. Now, in order to rebuild his confidence, he needed to be sure of what the Lord's instructions were for transporting the Ark of God. Once he was confident in the proper procedures, that confidence completely exuded from King David. He and all Israel sang praises and made music with horns, trumpets, cymbals and stringed instruments as the Ark entered the City of David.

David's confidence, shown through his praise and thanksgiving and dancing before the Lord, offended some, namely his discontented wife, Michal, the daughter of Saul. With that said, be humbly confident and rejoice in the knowledge that God has given you. On the other hand, be aware of those who will despise you and be jealous of your freedom. Keep your friends close and your enemies even closer, aka: frienemies.

Zealous Enthusiasm

Genuine enthusiasm is not a lukewarm response! Revelation 3:16 says, "So then, because you are lukewarm, and neither cold nor hot, I will vomit you out of My mouth." The Lord isn't looking for a lukewarm Christian, and neither is your client looking for a lukewarm product, a lukewarm service, or a lukewarm person to do business with. It's exciting to do business with people who are excited. Don't let your circumstances affect your enthusiasm for what you do.

Indecision or apathy can be overcome by enthusiasm and enthusiasm is generally aroused by two things: 1) An idea that takes the imagination by storm and; 2) A definite and intelligible plan for carrying that ideal into practice. Put them both to work for you.

Seeing someone completely enthusiastic about a product is one of the best selling tools! As you generate excitement about your product or service, you begin to remove uncertainty that your client might have that you or your product may not be their best solution. The easiest way to become enthusiastic is to actually believe in your product yourself! Clients will naturally feed off your enthusiasm when it is genuine. What's even better is when you take that a step further and create an environment where clients can feed off of each other's enthusiasm! This is best when done in person. But, it can also be accomplished through your website, blog postings, social media or conference call forums.

If you're not going to show enthusiasm, chances are neither will your clients. Make it a point to make it easy for clients to get excited. Excitement sells!

Knowledge is power, but without action it is a waste. Don't get so caught up in over thinking, over deliberating or over researching that you fail to take any action. Procrastination and lack of implementation both kill!

"But be doers of the word, and not hearers only, deceiving yourselves...
For faith without works is dead." -James 1:22 & 2:20

Take, for example, the story out of 2 Samuel 20 when Sheba, the Benjamite, rebelled against King David. Trouble was about to break out and King David gave specific instructions to Amasa, his newly appointed commander, to assemble the men of Judah within three days. The Scriptures tell us that Amasa set out to assemble the men, however he took longer than the appointed time. The result: He was struck in the stomach by the sword of Joab and left for dead.

Often times people don't do things because they want to, but they do things because they have to. The same truth applies to the spiritual realm. You don't get spiritual because you want to; you get spiritual because you have to. Even the disciples fell into this boat. They did not leave Jerusalem and fulfill the great commission (Matthew 28:18-20) to make disciples of all people when they were told to. They stayed right where they were. It wasn't until they were driven out by persecution that they began to fulfill the call. God turned their procrastination into persecution, which drove them into obedience. Praise God for that persecution, lest His gospel message may never have reached you.

Be diligent to respond to the call. Pursue excellence and put faith into action within your business. Don't let procrastination kill you, your business, your dreams or your visions.

Responding to the call, whatever that call may be, is really a two-step process. Step one: Be prepared and properly equipped before you are called to action. Step two: Respond with obedience when you are called to action. The Scriptures are loaded with many examples of this two-step process.

Nehemiah is a great example of this principle. His call was to return to Jerusalem and rebuild the city walls, which were destroyed after the fall of Jerusalem. Step 1: He went out by night and surveyed the land. He gathered all the information necessary to formulate a plan of action. Step 2: When it was time to arise and build, he implemented that plan. This led to the amazing feat of rebuilding the city walls in an unprecedented fifty-two days.

It's a whole lot easier to implement a plan of action, when you've done the research necessary to know what to implement. Research comes in many forms. You might need to be like Nehemiah, and do your research in undetectable solitude. You may need to be like King David and search through written instructions for answers. Maybe you need to be an understudy like Elisha, and patiently follow in the footsteps of another man. As an understudy, be ready when the mantle drops, because it requires the action of your stooping down to pick it up.

"Ask, and it will be given to you; seek, and you will find; knock, and it will be opened to you." -Matthew 7:7

Overcoming Objections

Overcoming objections requires one major skill. It is the art of listening! If you are more concerned about what you have to say, you will not be able to focus on what your client has to say. When given the opportunity, a client will tell you exactly what you need to know to lead him in the process of closing the sale.

Just Listen! It's really quite simple, listen attentively and isolate the objection. Sometimes your clients may reveal more to you in their body language than they do with their words. This means you need to listen with your eyes as well. Still at other times, they may communicate more in their tone of voice. This means you need to listen with your heart.

As easy as it sounds, listening doesn't come easy for everybody. For some individuals it may seem like second nature, yet for others it is a learned behavior that comes through much practice. If you're not sure if you are a good listener, ask your spouse. If that doesn't work, try asking your children. You may be in for a rude awakening.

If your feedback to that question was less than desirable, don't worry. Listening is a skill that can be learned. Even the prophet Samuel had to learn the art of listening. When Samuel was at a young age, the Lord called out to him, but Samuel struggled to understand what he was hearing. It was only after Eli, his spiritual father, gave him directions on how to listen and how to respond, that Samuel learned how to listen (1 Samuel 3:1-20). From that day forward, Samuel was established as a prophet of the Lord, for he spoke what he heard from the Lord and none of his words fell to the ground. That means that everything Samuel spoke came to pass. Praise God he learned how to listen.

Man is full of objections and God is full of overcoming responses. He overcomes ashes and worthlessness with beauty, mourning with joy and a spirit of heaviness with praise (Isaiah 61:3). He overcomes hunger and thirst with righteousness, the blind and the deaf with understanding, and the meek with boldness. He overcomes fear with faith, and He has ultimately overcome Satan by the blood of the Lamb and by the word of our testimony.

Considering God knows your every thought before you even think or say it, overcoming for Him is a piece of cake! The issue then becomes whether or not you heed His response. You must rely on your ability to listen attentively to the needs, wants and desires of your clients. Objections made by clients can easily be struck down with factual information. That information comes in the form of product knowledge as we've discussed thus far throughout this chapter. Being well versed, not only in your products, but also in similar products sold by competitors, will allow you to easily counter objections. When a prospect offers an objection or says "no," usually he is really telling you, "I need more information." It has been shown that the typical consumer will say "no," at least twice prior to making a purchase. Your job then becomes finding out the information that the client needs in order to make the decision to purchase.

Isolate: What Is The Client Really Asking Of You?
Is it style or color? Is it which model is available? Is it price? Is it functionality? Is it time? Is it quality? Is it durability or longevity? Is it value? Is another person's approval needed? Is it beneficial for them?

CHAPTER FIFTEEN:
The Power Of The Testimony

What is it about testimonials that make them so powerfully compelling? The simple answer is that most people want to go, do, buy, or eat where other people have gone, done, bought, or eaten. Experimenting with unchartered territory is not the typical consumer's first choice. If the experts say you are good, they are more willing to test that theory than to go out on a limb alone.

Testimonies can come in many different shapes and sizes. They can be written, spoken, or even just implied. They can have an impact when heard firsthand in person, secondhand from a friend, or just caught unknowingly from a recording. A testimony can consist of words, sounds, pictures, flavors, aromas, or a mixture of all of the above. Anytime they touch one of the five major senses, they generally carry some type of influential power. In this chapter of Pillar 3: Product Knowledge, we will unwrap the power of the testimony.

"But sanctify the Lord God in your hearts, and always be ready to give a defense to everyone who asks you a reason for the hope that is in you, with meekness and fear." -1 Peter 3:15

Walking Epistles
Indeed, there are epistles that are written on stones and tablets for others to read, but there is another type of epistle, a living epistle in you, an epistle of your testimony written on your heart that others may see and read. Do you not know that you are a walking epistle? Yes, in the spiritual sense, you are a walking epistle for Christ. But, like it or not, you are also a walking epistle for you company. What you do, what you say, and how you conduct yourself are all a part of the continual epistle being written

about you and your business on the hearts and minds of those you come in contact with. "Selah." It kinda makes you stop and think a little bit, doesn't it?

Therefore, conduct yourself in such a way that your epistle may be read by all without shame, not in the letter of the law, but in the spirit of the law. As a walking epistle, always be prepared to be the walking promotion of your faith-based company. Don't be shy about your business. Be proud of what you do and what God is doing through you and your company, in a humble sort of way, of course.

Paul says that a letter of commendation is not necessary for you when the living Word of God is reflected and proven in your character. Walk and speak with love, and let the Spirit bring liberty in what you preach. For it is the Spirit that does the unveiling, which transforms us into His image, from glory to glory (2 Corinthians 3:1-18).

"You are our epistle written in our hearts, known and read by all men; clearly you are an epistle of Christ, ministered by us, written not with ink but by the Spirit of the living God, not on tablets of stone but on tablets of flesh, that is, of the heart." -2 Corinthians 3:2-3

Letter Of Recommendation
The apostle Paul wrote that a letter of commendation (praise) wasn't necessary to validate who Christ is inside of you, and it really isn't required to validate who Christ is in your business either. On the other hand, Paul did write letters of recommendation for Titus, Timothy, Aquila and Priscilla, to name a few, when he was introducing them and establishing their proper positions to others. To those who have not yet heard, seen, or experienced the difference in your company, the testimony or recommendation of others can have a huge impact on your business. They cannot take your place as the walking epistle, but they can certainly add to it.

A letter of recommendation can either subtly suggest something or it can strongly urge something. To urge someone or something carries a little more weight than just recommending someone or something.

Paul often urged the brethren. He urged them to take nourishment (Acts 27:34). He urged them to note those who cause divisions (Romans 16:17).

He urged them to imitate him as he imitates Christ (1 Corinthians 4:15-16). He urged them to reaffirm their love (2 Corinthians 2:8). He urged them to help those who labor in the gospel (Philippians 4:3). And, Paul especially urged them to pray for him (Hebrews 13:18-19).

To urge or to recommend someone or something must come from the heart. If it is not genuine, it will be to no avail. This process cannot and should not ever be manipulated. The truth will always make its way to the surface. When clients recommend you to someone they know it is usually because they want that person to experience the same positive encounter that they experienced. Operate your business in such a way that it is natural and even unstoppable for your clients to tell others about you!

Just to bring the significance of this home even further, we've included a few letters of recommendation and appreciation for you to read for yourself. Do they make a difference? You be the judge.

To Jeff & Theresa (clients from Iowa),

Well, you've made it! Congratulations on this step in faith! I have really enjoyed working with you both with this new venture! I hope that training week was helpful information in multiple avenues. Please use tech support as often as you need it to shorten your learning curve! A Scripture that I think of pertaining to your new business is: Matthew 6:33, "But seek first the kingdom of God and His righteousness, and all these things shall be added to you." Keep me posted on the development of the business, and be sure and send before/after pictures! Please type me a letter outlining your experience with our company from first phone call until now.

Blessings,

Nick, Personal Business Advisor
The Master's Touch, Glendale Arizona

To Nick (TMT Business Advisor),

Everything went great from the first day we called to the last day of training. You and your team have been great – answering questions and really giving us a great start to our new business. I can't wait to get the equipment so we can get our cargo van all set up. I also have a new support team in the other owners that we trained with and some great new friends also. Our stay was great, the food was great and the shuttle service was great also. Tonight we reviewed some of our strategies to market our business and here is the list we are starting with...

Jeff & Theresa, New Business Owners
Dyersville, Iowa

To Josh & The Master's Touch Team,

I wanted to take a moment to say thank you. You were the key role in this life changing experience I decided to take. You were there from the first phone call and it's great to know I can still talk to you and count on you months later. This was a huge step in my life and I would not have done it if you were not there for me when I was in doubt. My life has changed for the better and business is not so bad either. I'm getting more clients each day and building a business that is fun and exciting. I have taken everything I learned at training and am applying it everyday. I actually love waking up and going to work. I am now keeping God in my life at work, at play, at home, everywhere! Training was incredible and I will never forget my experience at The Master's Touch. You work with a bunch of amazing people! I have never experienced a feeling like that before. The love that is in that building is unheard of and made me feel safe, peaceful, comforted and happy while I was there. God bless you and everyone at The Master's Touch for changing my life.

God Bless you,
Dino, New Business Owner

Testimony Binder

Gathering information is only as valuable as what you do with the information that you gather. Many clients might respond to your outstanding service by writing you a letter of appreciation or recommendation. It might make you feel good when you read it, but if you don't share it with others, it can become a stagnant piece of paper.

You might display a few of the most memorable and encouraging testimonies in a frame on the walls of your business. Keep in mind; however, if your business takes you into the field, you can't exactly take your wall display with you very easily. Create a binder to display the testimonies that you have received. This is a convenient and great way for your clients to hear, see, and read about you from the mouth of another.

"Let another man praise you, and not your own mouth; A stranger, and not your own lips." -Proverbs 27:2

It's encouraging to know what previous clients have to say about their experience with your company. Now on the other hand, if their feedback isn't favorable, that's a whole other issue you must deal with. We'll talk more about "Customer Service Resolutions" in Pillar 4: Disciplined Actions. As for right now, and for the sake of argument, let's say the feedback is good. People want to know what other people have to say about you.

One important thing to keep in mind: you cannot please all of the people all of the time. However, don't let that discourage you from pleasing most of the people most of the time, because your competition is likely only pleasing some of the people some of the time.

A binder of testimonies can be more than just words. In fact, a picture speaks louder than a thousand words! A true, unaltered picture is without hypocrisy and without divination. It simply states and shows the facts for others to see and judge for themselves. If the nature of your business provides a service with definite before and after results, then let those results speak for themselves. Include before and after pictures in your binder. Tell about where and how different jobs were done, and how the results were achieved. Include photos of clients next to their letters of appreciation or recommendation (with their permission of course). Clients want to be able to relate to other clients. If your target market is housewives, they would most likely appreciate the testimony of another housewife, such as themselves, over an exquisitely typed letter from the Chairman of the Board of a fancy corporation that has nothing to do with them or their personal needs. It may give credibility to the matter, but it doesn't create the same relate-ability.

Social media is another form of vast communication that is sweeping our nation. Use it toward your advantage. Encourage you clients to post favorable feedback (with pictures if applicable) about their experience with your company. You might even ask them to tag their friends who they think would most benefit from your service or product. Word gets around real quick this way and it is most certainly contagious among social media fans.

Audio Video Testimonies
Use your website to its fullest potential. Text is necessary, but audio and visual elements are what capture people's attention. Having the right balance of all three of these elements makes for the most interactive website. Note: Interaction is a good thing here. For a great example of this principle in action, visit www.themasterstouch.net.

Audible testimonies have the unique ability to change how people see things. Take for example the story of Paul and his Damascus Road experience. Once he heard an "audible" from God, his entire testimony was about to do an about-face! It wasn't only an audible experience, but a visual experience as well.

As he was on his journey to persecute and arrest the Christians in Damascus, suddenly there appeared a blinding light from heaven. He fell to the ground, and heard a voice saying to him, "Saul, Saul, why are you persecuting Me?" And he said, "Who are You, Lord?" Then the Lord said, "I am Jesus, whom you are persecuting. It is hard for you to kick against the goads." (Acts 9:1-5) The testimony of Jesus has now affected Paul in a different and personal way. He never again would be the same.

An "audible" from you probably won't carry as much weight as an "audible" from God, but it will certainly make a difference. Even Christ said we would be able to do greater works than those seen by the disciples, if we would only believe.

Interactive Forums
An interactive forum offers your clients an opportunity to meet with each other and share ideas and views on a particular topic or issue. Oftentimes

the information exchanged in these settings proves invaluable to those attending. These forums can be done by way of Internet blogs, message boards, webinars (web seminar or conferencing), conference calls, in-store meetings, and the like.

Again we direct you to an example done through a faith-based company called The Master's Touch. The Master's Touch provides complete business package systems for the hard surface cleaning and restoration industry. Being that many, if not most, of their clients are new to the industry, there are many things to learn. Although extensive training is provided, some of the best advice can often come from a fellow business owner who has figured out simple tips and tricks of the trade. Such information is available through the company's organized biweekly conference calls. All business owners are invited to join in on the calls, where a specific topic is discussed and taught by one of their professional trainers, followed by business-owner input and interaction. This is a great example of taking advantage of interactive forums.

What do the Scriptures say about assembling together for such a purpose...

"And with many other words he testified and exhorted them, saying, 'Be saved from this perverse generation.' Then those who gladly received his word were baptized; and that day about three thousand souls were added to them. And they continued steadfastly in the apostles' doctrine and fellowship, in the breaking of bread, and in prayers." -Acts 2:40-42

"And let us consider one another in order to stir up love and good works, not forsaking the assembling of ourselves together, as is the manner of some, but exhorting one another, and so much the more as you see the Day approaching." -Hebrews 10:24-25

There is Biblical truth to the importance of creating forums for the interaction of clients and business owners. It is for the exhorting and encouraging of one another. This is the place where testimonies come alive when they operate in a spirit of love and cooperation and not in a spirit of murmuring and complaining. Like all things in your business, even the good things can become tainted if not kept in check. Be diligent to monitor for any bad apples, as they can spoil the whole bunch if left unchecked.

Ask For It

What are you doing to generate testimonials in your business? Most small business owners never ask for a testimonial, and even fewer yet seek them out with thank you letters or have their sales staff or service technicians ask, "How did I do?" If you just start asking, you might very well be amazed at what you receive.

When asking for a testimonial from your clients, there are a few things to go after that will help set a great testimony apart from a good testimony.

1. Use guiding questions to elicit specific answers when you send out your "thank you" letters. Every client should receive a "thank you" letter within 24 to 72 hours, no exceptions!

2. Acquire specific, detailed information; not just, "You were great." What made the experience great? Did you under promise and over deliver?

3. Identify your testimonies. Who are they from, what do they do, what town do they live in, what do they look like. All of these add credibility to your testimony.

4. Fact: Nurses and school teachers are considered the most trusted professions in the country. If you've served one of these, ask them for their testimony.

5. Use photos whenever possible. Ask clients if they have a photo of themselves that they particularly like, or be prepared to take one on the spot with their permission.

6. Use before and after pictures of services performed along with your clients' testimony, if that feature applies to your business.

7. Offer something to your clients for taking the time to give you their testimony. It could be a gift card to someplace they'd enjoy, or maybe a discount off their next service or purchase.

Take another look at the sample letters included just back a few pages. Did you notice how the testimonies were asked for by the business advisor in conjunction with the "thank you" letter that was sent out immediately following their experience? "Immediate" is the key word here. Kindly ask the clients to share their testimonies with you while the experience is still fresh in their minds.

Finish The Race!

So now what? You have two choices. You can be like the average person who goes through a workshop and gets excited temporarily, but does little or nothing to make any significant changes in himself or his company. Or, you can resolve to continue to review, practice and improve upon yourself and your business through what you've learned in the David's 400 curriculum.

What you focus on, you inevitably become more like. When you focus on marketing, marketing is what will increase. When you focus on customer service, client satisfaction will increase. If it is research and development, then innovations will be birthed. If your focus is on aligning your faith-based company with God's Word, then indeed blessings will come forth! Where your attention goes from here will direct where and how your company grows now and in the future. This would be a great time to stand on the promise of God's Word from Matthew 13:23; "But he who received seed on the good ground is he who hears the Word and understands it, who indeed bears fruit and produces: some a hundredfold, some sixty, some thirty."

Each day you must resolve to commit and re-commit yourself to your faith walk, to your spouse, to your family, and to your business. The important thing is to keep it in that order; notice that business isn't first on that list! Seek first the kingdom of God and all these things shall be added unto you (Matthew 6:33).

If you have been ministered to through this teaching, then you have most certainly been called to fight the good fight of faith... to press forward to that upward call of God in Christ Jesus... to finish the race!

PILLAR 4: DISCIPLINED ACTIONS

CHAPTER SIXTEEN:
Discipline Is A Choice

"See then that you walk circumspectly, not as fools but as wise, redeeming the time because the days are evil." -Ephesians 5:15-16

To walk circumspectly literally means to look around, or to be vigilant, keeping watch for possible danger or difficulties. As entrepreneurs and business owners, you are required to maintain a higher level of discipline and greater awareness of what's going on around you and your business. To whom much is given, much is required, and in like manner, with higher levels, come higher devils. This means you need to remain alert and attentive to what's happening in your business and in your home. Keep in mind, your home precedes your business and oftentimes it can be a reflection of what is taking place in your business.

The early Christians were called "disciples." Why? Because they were disciplined learners with disciplined actions. They no longer ran in the same flood of dissipation they used to, but led a disciplined life. Not a life full of rules and regulations, but a life of faith that was evidenced by their decency and order. The faith-based company would do well to follow the examples laid out before them by these pioneers. Among the top priorities of disciplined actions that new business owners ought to exercise are: prioritization, implementation, and consistency. Each of these topics and more will be expanded on in this chapter of Disciplined Actions.

Discipline is a choice. To achieve a level of success in anything in life requires a level of discipline. The level of success you achieve can largely be attributed to the corresponding level of discipline you exhibit in the area you are striving to be successful. Paul gives us a wonderful analogy in his first letter to the Corinthian church...

"Do you not know that those who run in a race all run, but one receives the prize? Run in such a way that you may obtain it. And everyone who competes for the prize is temperate in all things. Now they do it to obtain a perishable crown, but we for an imperishable crown. Therefore I run thus: not with uncertainty. Thus I fight: not as one who beats the air. But I discipline my body and bring it into subjection, lest, when I have preached to others, I myself should become disqualified." -1 Corinthians 9:24-27

Paul was saying that, in order to run with the objective of winning the race, to fight with the intention of actually striking and defeating his opponent, he must discipline his body and bring it into subjection, making the choice to first discover the necessary skills he would need in order to achieve success, and then making the continual choice to practice those same things so as to sharpen the skills he's learned so that when the time comes, they can be put into practical application and bring about the victory.

In order to run a successful business with a spirit of discipline, you must first identify two important things about yourself and your business... One: Areas of Weakness. Two: Areas of Strength.

Once identified, you must learn how to improve in both areas so that your areas of weakness will not cause you to fail, and that your areas of strength can lead you into the crown of success. Once you learn how you can improve in those areas, you must make the choice to put into action the very things that will help you improve. You must bring your actions into subjection and make the choice to be disciplined. Everything comes down to a choice, you can choose to be disciplined and prepare for eventual success, or make the choice to be lazy, and prepare for eventual defeat. Make no mistake; not making the choice to be disciplined is making the choice to be lazy. Proverbs 12:24 puts it this way, "The hand of the diligent will rule, but the lazy man will be put to forced labor."

Memorization With A Purpose

The act of memorizing anything takes a distinct and deliberate effort! Even for most individuals, their favorite song or a catchy jingle has to enter their ear more than once to really sink in. When it comes to memorization, repetition is the school master. Dictionary.com defines memorization as: to commit to memory; to learn by heart.

When you stop and think about it, the things you often learn by heart as kids are the things that continue to stay with you as adults. Most grown individuals in this country went through the process of memorizing their ABC's along with addition, subtraction and multiplication tables, not to mention, "I before E except after C." These are all necessary and valuable basics to retain in life. However, there is an even greater basic that you ought to learn by heart. It is God's living, powerful, written Word! Why should you memorize God's Word? Here are six simple answers in a nutshell...

1. Because He commands you to (Deuteronomy 11:18-22; Psalm 119:15-16; Philippians 4:6-8).

2. To help in times of temptation (Psalm 119:11; Matthew 4:4, 4:7, 4:10).

3. To make your way prosperous (Psalm 1:1-3; Joshua 1:8; Jeremiah 15:16).

4. To prepare your response to the world (Proverbs 13:4, 15:28; 1 Peter 3:15).

5. Because it is your shield and defense (Proverbs 30:5; Psalm 3:3; Ephesians 6:10-18).

6. It is how you walk by faith (Habakkuk 2:4; Romans 1:17; Hebrews 10:35-38; 2 Timothy 4:7-8).

Do you realize how much of God's Word you could hide in your heart if you only put to memory one new Scripture each week... That's fifty-two in just one year. This one act of discipline may very well change your life!

"Your Word I have hidden in my heart, that I might not sin against You."
-Psalm 119:11

Visit davids400.com for more information or to obtain your own copy of an entire year worth of Scripture memory verses in a handy organized flip chart. Or if memorizing is easier for you through the ear gate, we have a tool for that as well. Each of the fifty-two Scriptures have been conveniently recorded on an audio CD to aid you in the memorization process. Faith comes by hearing and hearing by the Word of God (Romans 10:17). The more you hear something, the more you get it. No more excuses not to!

CHAPTER SEVENTEEN:
Setting Proper Priorities

The Importance Of Prioritizing
Without setting proper priorities, it's easy to let your day get carried off with the wind, going to and fro, without any real direction. Many people don't really know exactly where their time and energy go each day because it's nearly impossible to mentally track each and every activity they do.

Homework Assignment
If you were to track your moment-by-moment activities, it might be a real eye-opening experience. It would certainly help you recognize what your habits and trends are. Try it for a day. Just simply keep a notepad with you at all times and record what you've done and how long it took. This includes recording such things as how long it takes you to get ready in the morning, or how long you watch TV or how long you spend in idle chit chat. It will be interesting to see what things literally eat up your time and interrupt your priorities. If you're honest with this assignment, you'll have an accurate history of which types of activities consumed your time and energy throughout the day and what areas need serious attention.

Once you have a better understanding of this, it will be easier to move on to setting realistic goals for prioritizing the most valuable resources you have: your time, your talent, and your treasure.

Prioritizing Your Time
For most, disciplining your time requires the chastening of your flesh. "Now no chastening seems to be joyful for the present, but painful; nevertheless, afterward, it yields the peaceable fruit of righteousness to those who have been trained by it." (Hebrews 12:11) And, again in Proverbs 3:12 and Hebrews 12:6, the same principle is admonish.... "For whom the Lord loves He corrects." Managing your time, setting priorities, and implementing your strategies require consistent disciplined actions.

We will start with a simple exercise, and then work into more detailed exercises and examples as we continue in this chapter. Keep in mind as you go, should you not feel like doing any of the exercises that is your choice. However, disciplining yourself (your flesh) to complete them will be to your greatest advantage. Whoever said discipline was easy? Certainly not the Scriptures!

Choose & Arrange

The first place to start is to choose and write down your goals and priorities on paper. This should align with your vision statement and your core principles written from previous exercises. Step two is to arrange them according to priority of importance or time sensitivity. Step three is to concentrate on the most vital priorities first. Give attention to quick deadlines and items that carry the most important weight in your business. Note: you must be sensitive to discern the true priority of things. One of the top time-wasters is often interruptions or activities that draw away your attention as if they were urgent, but in actuality they were not urgent at all.

Prioritizing your tasks into one of the four following categories can help you manage your time more efficiently. One: vital and urgent. Two: vital but not urgent. Three: urgent but not vital. Four: not vital and not urgent.

Implementing Time Priorities

So you have chosen the activities for your day and you've arranged them according to importance and urgency. So now the question becomes, "What is really on your plate today?" Implementing the priorities for your day requires two key elements: focus and flexibility.

No matter how hard you focus on your set activities for the day, you must be prepared to operate with a spirit of flexibility. Godly flexibility is when you flex with God's plans in lieu of your own, not compromising His agenda in lieu of your own ideals. With that in mind, here are a few things to consider when focusing with flexibility on your agenda for the day.

Make a set appointment each day (early in the day) to spend at least 15-20 minutes planning and prioritizing your day.

Use the essential planning and prioritizing guidelines. Decide which activities are absolute necessities for the day. Schedule and do them as early in the day as possible.

Be efficient. Group like objects together for maximum efficiency and decide what time of day is the most practical time to accomplish these activities.

Work in waves of energy to maximize your time, intense concentration efforts followed by short recovery periods of simple tasks.

Set the right environment and remove clutter and other distractions from your workspace.

Control interruptions, but make allowance for them to occur. Never plan your day so tightly that there is no room for spontaneity. Plan for the unexpected to happen.

Be proactive but be reasonable not to over extend yourself, it only creates chaos.

Wise Stewardship Over Your Time
Excellence requires wise stewardship over our time. To some, this may involve more than you think. It is important to understand that there are two distinctly different types of time, one is "chronos" time, the other is "kairos" time. Chronos time is quantity time or chronological order of time. Kairos time is quality time or an appointed time; set or divine opportunities; set times occurring inside of or during chronos time.

Chronos & Kairos Time
You are to walk diligently in the chronos time, being prepared to act upon the kairos moments placed before you. When a great and effective door opens up to you, understand, there will be adversaries. Don't let worry, doubt and fear keep you from opportune times. The truth is; if you don't do it, no one else will do it the same way you would have done it. The banner verse for this pillar says, "See then that you walk circumspectly, not as fools but as wise, redeeming the time because the days are evil." This "time" is in reference to kairos time. We all have the same gift of time (chronos) given to us, therefore, how you use it or how you redeem it is what sets you and your faith-based company apart. When the Scripture says, "See that you walk..." It is referring to how you mentally discern or take heed to the conduct of yourself in those moments of time.

Prioritizing Your Talent
Talent, by definition, refers to someone's natural aptitude or skill. Some may be exceptionally talented or incredibly gifted with distinct abilities, but

that doesn't negate the fact that everyone has been given some type of talent or ability to function in life. A man or woman may make mistakes and have imperfections but can still walk in a spirit of excellence. Excellence is not a downward spiral of misused talents, but rather the state of an upward climbing heart posture. Misusing the talents that God has given you is not something to take lightly. When he has given you the ability to use your talent to turn a profit, then that is exactly what you are to do! Why? Not for selfish gain, but to bring in provision for the kingdom of God. We'll expand on that subject in the following pages. For now, let's take a look at a talent that often gets overlooked. It's the talent or gift of hearing.

"For whoever has, to him more will be given, and he will have abundance; but whoever does not have, even what he has will be taken away from him. Therefore I speak to them in parables, because seeing they do not see, and hearing they do not hear, nor do they understand." -Matthew 13:12-13

"Also He said to them, 'Is a lamp brought to be put under a basket or under a bed? Is it not to be set on a lamp stand? For there is nothing hidden which will not be revealed, nor has anything been kept secret but that it should come to light. If anyone has ears to hear, let him hear.' Then He said to them, 'Take heed what you hear. With the same measure you use, it will be measured to you; and to you who hear, more will be given. For whoever has, to him more will be given; but whoever does not have, even what he seems to have will be taken from him.' " -Mark 4:21-25

In both examples from Matthew and Mark, Christ is speaking about the talent or gift of hearing and understanding. "He who has ears to hear let him hear!" (Matt 13:9). Hearing ears are an essential need for a teachable heart. Approximately one-third of Jesus' teaching was in parables; brief stories from everyday life told by way of analogy to illustrate spiritual truths. Their purpose was to make spiritual truths more clear to those who heard and to declare judgment upon those who were willfully blind.

Those who have already shut their eyes and ears to the truth will not realize the significance of what they are seeing and hearing, and consequently will not repent and receive forgiveness. Those who have ears will seek to understand the lessons taught by parables, or will be stimulated to probe for deeper understanding. Jesus exhorts them to hear and to heed His admonition for spiritual perception. Those who receive and assimilate the truth have their capacity for understanding enlarged and their knowledge increased. Those who disbelieve or are indifferent will lose whatever ability for understanding they had, and, therefore, will continue in ignorance.

Use It Or Lose It!

This principle can be applied to your business as well as your everyday life. Are you really listening to what is going on in your business? Are you listening with your eyes, your ears, and your heart? If the Lord has given you a heart that perceives, for God's sake, don't waste it! Discern what is going on around you. How does it align with God's Word? What actions need to be taken, or refrained from being taken? You can't expect to find guiding answers if you're not paying attention to the true nature of things.

Unlike man's subjective perspective, God's perspective is objective and redeeming. To him who hears, the Holy Spirit desires to give God's Biblical perspective. Biblical perspective allows you to give thanks for what you do have rather than complain about what you don't have.

Wise Stewardship Over Your Talent

What is God's will for you? You are called to walk by faith. When you're not sure how, just do what you know how to do until God reveals the next step. If you are not called or you do not have confirmation on doing something, play it safe, don't do it! The steps of a righteous man are directed by the Lord, not by your own opinion. The key lesson: Operate within your God given post!

King Saul learned this lesson the hard way. The people wanted a king, so God sent Samuel the prophet to anoint Saul the king over Israel. At that time, Samuel had given Saul specific instructions. Did he follow them? Not quite. Notice that Saul was anointed king, not priest. When Saul was on the battlefront with the Philistines, he became worried about what he should do, so he decided to offer up a sacrifice to the Lord. The problem with that is that was the responsibility of the priest, not the king. Rather than waiting for Samuel, Saul presumed to operate in a position outside of his God given post.

Want to know what that presumptive move cost him? The kingdom! Saul was appointed and anointed with the talents he needed to operate as a king. He was not called to offer up sacrifices and move in the role of what was exclusively reserved for the priests of Levi at that time in history.

Know what your talents and gifts are and operate in them. If you have difficulties balancing your own checkbook, then you have no business trying to balance your corporate figures. Hire someone with the gift to do it for you.

On the other hand, you may have the ability to do multiple facets of your organization. But, in respect to what your time and talent is worth, prioritize the things that you really excel in. You may be well able to write informative columns about your industry, but if it takes you two hours, and your staff member can do just as good a job in forty-five minutes, then delegate the task and stay on-point with your most personally effective talents.

As previously mentioned excellence mandates discipline. It takes discipline to stay at your post and on target. The result of this kind of disciplined life yields the fruit of excellence both in your business and in your personal life. Beware though, for discipline involves warfare. Satan doesn't want Jesus to get the glory, and he'll continue to battle over it. Victory requires continual discipline over your time, your talent, and your treasure that is mixed with obedient faith.

Prioritizing Your Treasure
In order to prioritize your treasure, it would seem you'd have to know what your treasure is. For some, it is real simple. It is their wealth or their finances. However, to others it may be their health or their vitality, and to others, still, it may be their accomplishments. Whatever the treasure, it is something that you personally consider valuable or precious. In Psalm 135, God refers to His chosen people as His special treasure and His precious possession. The book of Proverbs has a plethora of tidbits regarding treasure. Let's take a look at a few...

"In the house of the righteous there is much treasure, but in the revenue of the wicked is trouble." -Proverbs 15:6

"Better is a little with the fear of the Lord, than great treasure with trouble." -Proverbs 15:16

"There is desirable treasure, and oil in the dwelling of the wise, but a foolish man squanders it." -Proverbs 21:20

"How much better to get wisdom than gold! And to get understanding is to be chosen rather than silver." -Proverbs 16:16

Wise Stewardship Over Your Treasure
For the sake of argument, let's consider your treasure as the financial responsibility bestowed upon you and your business. When God has given you the ability to use your time and your talents to create a profit with the treasures you have, that is exactly what He expects. We'll be looking at the parable of the talents in Matthew, Chapter 25 for a depiction of this principle. The story opens with a man who is traveling to a far country. Before he journeys, he leaves something with each of his three servants.

"And to one he gave five talents, to another two, and to another one, to each according to his own ability; and immediately he went on a journey. Then he who had received the five talents went and traded with them, and made another five talents. And likewise he who had received two gained two more also. But he who had received one went and dug in the ground, and hid his lord's money." (Vs. 15-18)

"When the man returned he sought an account for the money he entrusted to his servants. To the two servants who had doubled the money, the man was well pleased... Well done, good and faithful servant; you were faithful over a few things, I will make you ruler over many things. Enter into the joy of your lord." (Vs. 21 & 23)

"But to the other who was afraid and hid the money and profited him nothing he said... You wicked and lazy servant, you knew that I reap where I have not sown, and gather where I have not scattered seed. So you ought to have deposited my money with the bankers, and at my coming I would have received back my own with interest. So take the talent from him, and give it to him who has ten talents. For to everyone who has, more will be given, and he will have abundance; but from him who does not have, even what he has will be taken away. And cast the unprofitable servant into the outer darkness. There will be weeping and gnashing of teeth." (Vs. 26-30)

Watchfulness does not mean idleness, but rather a faithful discharge of one's responsibilities. The wise use of gifts and abilities entrusted to you results in greater opportunities, while their neglect results not only in the loss of more or other opportunities, but also the loss of that which was entrusted to you in the first place. In this parable, there is quite a contrast between the reward of further responsibilities to the diligent servant, and judgment and loss to the inactive and lazy servant. The faithful discharge of the responsibilities God has given you is no joke. Don't make the mistake of taking it lightly, lest it cost you everything, including your business.

The David's 400 curriculum is packed full of Biblical principles that will aid in the generation of profits for your company. Will you put them to use like the wise servant, expecting the double portion as a result? Or will you dig a hole in the ground or hide them in the back of your closet, allowing fear to rule over you and keep you from prospering according to the abilities God has given you? We hope your answer is the former and not the latter!

This brings us to another point. What is the appropriate distribution of the treasure generated by your business? The answer for the faith-based company will differ from that of the world's common corporation, and we preface our response with the disclaimer that, "you are to work out your own salvation with fear and trembling." (Philippians 2:12) In other words, be obedient to your conscience and let the Holy Spirit convict you on the details. It may not be the same for everyone. However, there is one thing that we know for sure... The tithe belongs to the Lord!

The most common response to that declaration is, "Do you tithe on the gross or the net?" Again, you work it out with fear and trembling. One thing to keep in mind is that God allowed you the ability to generate 100% of it. Now if you choose to give the government the first cut and God the second cut, that's up to you. Jesus responded to this same concern by the Pharisees. His response, "Render to Caesar the things that are Caesar's, and to God the things that are God's." (Matt 22:21 & Mark 12:17)

"Honor the Lord with your possessions, and with the firstfruits of all your increase; So your barns will be filled with plenty, and your vats will overflow with new wine." -Proverbs 3:9-10

Store Up Treasures In Heaven
This principle is not about storing up good works or giving money in order to secure a place in heaven. It's really much deeper than that. To get to the root of what Christ is saying you must understand the context

and definition of the words that He is speaking. We will approach this by exegeting the Scriptures in reference to how difficult it is for a rich man to enter the kingdom of God. Starting with Matthew 19:21-22; "Jesus said to him, 'If you want to be perfect, go, sell what you have and give to the poor, and you will have treasure in heaven; and come, follow Me.' But when the young man heard that saying, he went away sorrowful, for he had great possessions."

Because of certain language barriers, the true meaning of this verse reads a bit differently than the traditional interpretation. Here it is in the literal English translation...

"If you take pleasure in being mature with human integrity and need nothing to be complete, then go barter, trade and sell what you have. Take your possessions, your wealth and your unnecessary acquisitions and supply them to those who are poor and unable to accomplish much of anything. Trade your earthly excess goods to those who are destitute of Christian values and eternal riches, having no interest of spiritual treasures. For then you shall lay hold in your hand and posses in your mind the spiritual faculties, virtues and thankfulness of one living in constant heartfelt union with Christ. Opportunities and advantages will be made available for your enjoyment and use. A heavenly place shall be appointed for your future abode along with those whom God has given eternal salvation, whose names have been written in the Lamb's book of life. A special place has been reserved for those who respond to the urgent and immediate calling to come alongside as a wholly conforming disciple of Christ."

The young ruler was unable to follow, for the possessions of his wealth were wrapped up and firmly secured in the possessions of his mind. Do you see the significance in what is actually being said? Get rid of the excess junk you don't need. Let it weigh and burden the heathen down; allow the proceeds to benefit the kingdom of God. In exchange for that, you shall receive a hundredfold in this life and eternal life to come, however, it will come with persecutions (Mark 10:29-30).

"Then Jesus said to His disciples, 'Assuredly, I say to you that it is hard for a rich man to enter the kingdom of heaven. And again I say to you, it is easier for a camel to go through the eye of a needle than for a rich man to enter the kingdom of God.' When His disciples heard it, they were greatly astonished, saying, 'Who then can be saved?' But Jesus looked at them and said to them, 'With men this is impossible, but with God all things are possible.' " -Matthew 19:23-26

According to man's standards, it's impossible to give away the farm and still stay in business. But, with God, all things are possible! Operating your business with a genuine spirit of giving is what keeps you afloat. Actually, it does more than keep you afloat, it's what puts the wind in your sails. Mixed with faith, it is the driving force of Christianity and the proof text of the Spirit in you. If you really want to store up treasures in heaven, then start giving things away! It is the universal law of seed faith. You must sow a seed in order to reap a harvest, and with the same measure that you sow, it will be measured back to you.

As mentioned earlier, being a wise steward over your treasure requires action not idleness. Actions that will create profits, actions that will double your investments, actions that are willing to give, and let go of earthly possessions for the benefit and advantage of others.

Look for the kairos moment of opportunities to give! Generously give to your clients, to your staff, to your family, to your church, to your community, and to people you do not know, or may never see again. Giving need not have boundaries, but it should be done with discernment, i.e. giving a homeless person on the street money is not the wisest gift, but rather a stumbling block that might enable him to buy more dope, more booze, or more of whatever his vice is. Instead, give them packaged food or clothing to provide for his needs not his wants.

"Do not lay up for yourselves treasures on earth, where moth and rust destroy and where thieves break in and steal; but lay up for yourselves treasures in heaven, where neither moth nor rust destroys and where thieves do not break in and steal. For where your treasure is, there your heart will be also." -Matthew 6:19-21

CHAPTER EIGHTEEN:
Systems & Implementations

There are a variety of systems that you may need to implement in your new business in order to operate at your fullest potential. Some of which might include systems for maintaining and operating your equipment, systems for managing your leads, systems for tracking your financial books, systems for accommodating quality service, systems for resolving mishaps, systems for obtaining client feedback, and so on...

Setting goals and writing down your vision is a vital part of business, but without systems to support them, they become hard to reach. For many entrepreneurs, systems become the heart of their business. An effective system is built from a variety of sub-systems that each operates in its unique function. These can include elements such as technical skills, accountability skills, intellectual skills, communication skills, trouble-shooting skills, and so forth, each one working together to create a greater whole.

One key thing to remember here: the implementation of any system requires consistent discipline in order to be effective. Even the best system is only as good as the one who works it. You might have the most phenomenal quality assurance system in your industry, but if you fail to implement it, it avails you nothing. In the following chapter, we will cover a few strategies for designing, writing, promoting, and following effective systems for your faith-based company.

Business Operations
There are many things to consider when operating a business, and certainly some more than others. It is important to consider not only what needs to be done but also who will be doing what. What things will you do yourself, and what things will require additional assistance? Make a list that identifies as many details as you can think of which relates to your specific business.

From that list, an operations or employee flowchart can prove helpful to organizing staff responsibilities and operations.

The flowchart is a means of visually presenting the flow of data for any given procedure or operation. Flowcharts may include the operations performed within a system, the sequence in which they are performed, and how or who will be performing them.

The chain of command ought to begin with the CEO, then to the team captains, then down to the additional staff members throughout each of the corporation's departments. Setting a chain of command in place began back in Biblical times. Moses and King David, as well as many other great leaders knew and understood the benefit of setting captains over captains.

"And Moses chose able men out of all Israel, and made them heads over the people: rulers of thousands, rulers of hundreds, rulers of fifties, and rulers of tens. So they judged the people at all times; the hard cases they brought to Moses, but they judged every small case themselves." -Exodus 18:25-26

"And David numbered the people who were with him, and set captains of thousands and captains of hundreds over them." -2 Samuel 18:1

Customer Service Blueprint
Now that you know who is in charge of specific details, it's time to focus on achieving customer service excellence. The objective of the "customer service blueprint" is to design a step-by-step process that consistently delivers excellence, and accommodates your clients in a way that meets or exceeds their needs and expectations. It's hard to deliver service excellence without first understanding and designing the process for which you will be accommodating the customer.

There are four key elements to keep in mind when drafting a customer service blueprint for your business. Regardless of the nature of your business, each of these will apply.

Design: Understand the optimal agenda you want your clientele to experience with your company.

Write: Put this ideal into a clearly defined step-by-step process; first greeting to final delivery.

Promote: Assign each sequence of events to team members most gifted in each specific activity.

Follow: The plan is only as good as the team who enthusiastically puts it in place. Consequences and rewards may be helpful motivators.

"Set your business in order, arrange your work in the fields; afterward you may build up your house." -Proverbs 24:27 (AAT)

Step One: Design
The best starting point of understanding the service process is to think of it as a commodity. The commodity of excellent service has value just like any other product sold. However, this commodity of value is often overlooked, perhaps in part because of its unique features. Because of the intangible nature of service, our first challenge in designing a service plan is to make it more tangible. A tangible blueprint allows the team members involved in performing the service to know what type of experience they are to consistently create and deliver in order to fulfill the customer's expectations.

Designing a customer service blueprint for your business starts by creating a description of each individual event you plan to orchestrate as part of the total service experience from start to finish. Each event should be considered as a specialized service goal between you, your staff, and your clients. Begin your design from the moment you first greet your clients to the time you thank them and say good-bye. It's important that you leave no details undone in your specialized blueprint. Some events or activities in your plan may be more impressive than others, but we guarantee, it's the seemingly small details that will get the attention and be noticed most.

When first laying out your blueprint, it's easiest to break your design into sub-categories. The general steps first, then follow with the details to coincide with each step, and then who will be performing each specific event or activity. Remember, people do what you inspect not what you expect, so have a follow up plan in place to make sure all events and activities are being performed and completed as you have laid them out in your customer service blueprint.

Step Two: Write

Write it out! Systems allow ordinary people to do and predict extraordinary results. You'd be amazed at what you and your staff members are capable of with the proper system of organization in place. You might also be amazed at how quickly things can slip though the cracks without it! Take time to list each team member responsible for the specific event or activity your business intends to engage in with the client. Some activities may allow for more than just one team member's participation, and some activities may require everyone's participation.

Step Three: Promote

Now it's time to get your team actively participating! Your best performers will be: those who specifically know what you expect from them, and those who are placed in the area in which they are most naturally gifted. Each team member not only needs a copy of your company's customer service blueprint, but they also need to be informed and trained as to how their specific service responsibilities are to be performed. The key word here is train, train, and train! Excellence in service is more about how than about what. Train each team member of your staff to enrich every transaction or activity involving the client with the following relationship builders.

Connect! Connect with the client first before anything else. Promptly and genuinely welcome every client as though he was a guest in your home. If sitting, stand up to greet him.

Clarify! When you think you understand the wants or needs of your client, take time to repeat it back to him. If you've ever visited Carl's Jr. than you would know how well they have this step down.

Comply! When complying with a client request, it is vital to respond quickly. Clients want you to be prompt even though they may enjoy taking their own time.

Customize! Clients want and expect a degree of flexibility. Be willing and prepared to adjust to individual styles and requests.

Consistency! Consistency is crucial. When a service establishment is not consistent with service delivery, customers feel like they are being jerked back and forth like the tip of a fly rod.

Conclude! This is a critical element of service success. How you conclude will be the last thing on a client's mind. The last impression is the first thing he often tells his friends about. Make a statement of appreciation that lasts, and be sure to invite him back.

Step Four: Follow

Now that your team is fully trained on what and how your business will engage in its ideal of customer service excellence, it is time to make sure the "when" part gets done. No matter how fantastic your blueprint is on paper, it is only as good as the team who enthusiastically puts it into action. Miscommunication regarding who is responsible for getting things done, and when they are to be done, usually leads to things not getting done.

Since your when time is not set by a clock, but rather it varies from client to client and activity to activity, you will need a system in place which holds your team accountable. As stated previously, people will do what you inspect, not what you expect. Rewards, incentives, discipline, and consequences can be used as effective motivational tools in this area.

It is important, however, to consider that excellent customer service should be a standard expectation of all team members. It's kind of like brushing your teeth. It's a minimum expectation that should be performed each day, regardless whether you're told to or not. Does anyone really give you a prize when you do a great job brushing your teeth? Well, the answer is both "yes" and "no." Obviously, there is no tooth fairy standing by with a blue ribbon, but there is a dentist waiting by every six months with his fancy little drill when you do a poor job. So then, even regarding basic expectations there is a consequence, either good or bad, when things are or are not performed as they ought to be.

Incentives: What type of incentives or rewards are you willing to offer your staff for excellence accomplished in customer service? Consequences: What type of discipline or consequences will you have in place when excellence is not achieved or is neglected in the customer service plan?

The Resolution Process
Bringing yourself and your staff back into alignment is one thing, but what happens when you're out-of-whack with your clients? Sometimes things just don't go as planned. Every company needs to have some type of compliant resolution process in place, a process in which a resolution is established between the company and the consumer in the event of mishaps.

During the reign of King David, he foolishly decided to number the children of Israel, a direct violation of his covenant relationship with the Lord. His heart condemned him, then convicted him, and quickly repented him. God's resolution process for Israel consisted of giving King David a multiple choice solution. (A) 3 years of famine. (B) 3 months fleeing from his enemies. (C) 3 days of plague in the land.

Now, even though this example is about discipline for David's shortcomings, it can still be used in a positive way to accommodate your client as a result of any shortcomings on behalf of your company. Some restaurants and other establishments even post their policy right up front indicating their "quick-fix" resolution process.

"If you are not completely satisfied with your meal, we'll promptly make you another." or "If we fail to give you a receipt, your next meal is on us." or "If we overbook your flight, we'll send you on the next available flight and give you a travel voucher for $500 for any inconvenience we may have caused you."

It's a proven Biblical fact, "All have sinned and fall short of the glory of God" (Romans 3:23). When you know this, realize you're bound to make mistakes from time to time. How you handle these mistakes is what will make all the difference between the relationship you have and the relationship you keep with your clients and your business.

Minimizing Offenses
The Scriptures say that offenses must come, not that they are done intentionally, but things just happen. How you handle these offenses can either quench that offense or fuel it. When clients feel they have been wronged, mistreated, or had a breach in their contract, there are four basic, yet very important things they are looking for from you.

Recognize: They want to know that you have heard and understand the problem or situation.

Repent: Like it or not they expect an apology, go a step further and make sure it's sincere.

Reassure: Let them know the situation will be properly handled and avoided in future events.

Resolve: Use the multiple-choice, the quick-fix solution, or allow the client to suggest a suitable solution.

"Moreover if your brother sins against you, go and tell him his fault between you and him alone. If he hears you, you have gained your brother... Then Peter came to Him and said, 'Lord, how often shall my brother sin against me, and I forgive him? Up to seven times?' Jesus said to him, 'I do not say to you, up to seven times, but up to seventy times seven.' " -Matthew 18:15 & 21-22

The Collaborative Solution
Once you've been alerted to an issue, you've listened to the client's concerns, apologized with sincerity, and reassured him of a suitable solution, then it's time to follow through with the resolution process. You might organize a multiple choice option, such as the Lord did with King David in the previous example, or you may want to let the client suggest something. The latter choice of a collaborative solution is how King David handled the infraction, which occurred with the Gibeonites in 2 Samuel 21.

You see, back when Joshua was first conquering the Promised Land, he made a covenant (actually he was tricked into making a covenant, but we'll discuss that part later) with the Gibeonites swearing Israel's protection to them, but King Saul later sought to kill the Gibeonites in his own zeal. It later came to pass, that a famine was in the land because of Saul's ruthless killing of the Gibeonites. When David asked the Gibeonites, "What shall I do for you? And with what shall I make amends that you may bless the Lord's inheritance? (Forgive the wrong by Israel)." The Gibeonites did not want silver or gold, but they wanted the death of their descendants avenged by the death of seven of Saul's descendants. Difficult as it was,

David honored their request. Then God heard the prayer for the land, and the famine ceased, and the rains poured down.

Understand, that sometimes, as in this example, the corrective resolution you offer your clients isn't just for their appeasement and amends, but it's also for you and your needed forgiveness! David didn't personally kill the Gibeonites, but he represented the nation in whom their killer was a part. When your staff wrongs a client, whether by error or by omission, you, as the business owner, are still held responsible. It's your job to make it right!

"So they performed all that the king commanded. And after that God heeded the prayer for the land." -2 Samuel 21:14

Consistency Throughout Your Company
It's great when staff members can provide speedy resolutions to client issues. However, this can quickly go down hill if there is a lack of communication between departments. Suppose department "A" tells the client one thing and directs him to department "B" for his resolution, but "B" tells the client something different, you now may have a very disgruntled client on your hands. It is very frustrating when multiple staff members within the same organization all have different answers on how to handle the same issue. Make sure that each department is cross-trained with the other departments regarding its specific resolution process. Consistency within will help prevent this kind of unnecessary dissatisfaction.

Making Amends
Resolving mishaps with your staff or your clients is the simple process of making amends. The willingness to make minor changes in order to make things right will set you apart from the business owner who is only in it for himself. Be willing to humble yourself and acknowledge your mistakes, whether they are yours personally or that of your staff. Then, go to the Lord in meekness and ask for His direction and plans for corrections. The faith-based company is not afraid to make mid-course corrections!

Let's recap the three resolution processes we have covered...

The multiple-choice solution: Provide three suitable solutions for the client to choose one from. The quick-fix solution: Use the up-front concept; if we mess it up, we'll quickly fix it up. The collaborative solution: Let the client offer a suitable resolution to the situation. You may discover that often the client is less generous with his compensation idea than you would have been. Let your conscience be your guide on this one.

Satisfaction Guaranteed

If your aim is to guarantee satisfaction to your clients, then you'll need a system in place to measure that satisfaction. Certainly you can just simply ask your clients, "How have we done?" or, "Have we met all of your expectations?" However, with these types of questions, you're more likely to get a courtesy type of answer. If you want more of a well-thought-out answer, try asking, "How can we improve." Clients feel the least threatened and are the most open and honest when they can provide feedback in an anonymous way, unless of course you offer them incentives for responding to a survey.

If you are going to take the time to implement a survey in your business, make it worthwhile. Ask questions that really matter to you and your company. Make it easy for your client to respond. Ask questions that focus on the outstanding elements of your company, but be prepared to receive constructive criticism. Using a one to five type of grading scale traditionally works well, but always allow space for the client to express his own feedback. Keep in mind, you can please some of the people some of the time, but you won't please all of the people all of the time. Be open and use discernment when reviewing the completed surveys. How does the feedback align with your vision statement and the core principles for your company? You may need to activate your resolution process.

Surveys are not always about making changes or improvements. At times, they may be a word in due season, an encouragement just when you need it most (Proverbs 15:23). Share these exhortations with your staff that they also might share in the encouragement and reward of a job well done.

Satisfaction Survey Samples

Surveys can take on many forms. They often encompass questions about how your client perceives your product or how your service was provided. They can also be drafted in the form of a quiz, geared toward what the clients gained or remembered from their experience with you. Whatever system you implement, it's really about what provides you with the feedback necessary to monitor your service or product.

CHAPTER NINETEEN:
Consistency

There are many things that truly hold a company together, and consistency is definitely one of them. The Latin origin of the word consistency means to stand firm. So then, if faith is the backbone of your company, we'd dare to say that consistency is the blood that flows through it. Consistency allows you to stand firm in the results generated within you company. Without consistency it is difficult, if not impossible, for a company to work and flow in unity. If everyone is doing what is right in his own eyes based upon his own feelings, you will not and cannot walk in one accord!

Consistency in the business arena does not contain contradictions. It is the achievement of a level of performance that does not vary in quality over location, over provider, or over time. More than anything, consistency requires discipline. Disciplining yourself or your staff to do something once is worthy, but it carries little weight in comparison to doing something consistently with a spirit of excellence over and over again.

Get The Basics Right First
Paul wrote to the Romans that if the firstfruit is holy, the lump is also holy; and if the root is holy, so are the branches (Romans 11:16). If you are consistent in the small things, expect to be rewarded in the greater things (Matthew 25:21). However, if you can't master the basics, how do you plan to excel in the more advanced things? Repetition is the school master and consistency is her teacher. It's the small things consistently done right over time that make a big difference! The five foundational pillars of business taught within are the basics that must be done with purpose and consistency. They are the building blocks of the faith-based company! Let's recap...

Pillar 1: Building Relationships. Be consistent in building genuine relationships with your clients and your staff. Consistently differentiate and correlate your product or service with your target market. Keep consistent communication between you, your staff, and your client.

Pillar 2: Seed Time & Harvest. Be consistent at sowing seeds into good ground, expecting a harvest to come. Consistently monitor and measure your advertising campaigns. Keep consistent repeat and referral programs in place and active. Always operate in a spirit of giving.

Pillar 3: Product Knowledge. Be consistent in your pursuit for excellence, not perfection. Consistently equip yourself and your staff with firsthand knowledge. Consistently operate in a spirit of humble confidence and zealous enthusiasm. Always present yourself as the walking epistle of your faith-based company.

Pillar 4: Disciplined Actions. Be consistent in setting priorities with your time. Be consistent to operate in the post in which God has placed you. Consistently be a wise steward over the resources God has given you. Be consistent with your systems and their implementation.

Pillar 5: Flee Idleness. Lead your staff and your clients with consistent values and godly principles. Consistently surround yourself with dynamic team players. Stay consistent in the management of day-to-day business operations. Always apply the 72 hour rule for any major decision.

The 5 Pillars Of Faith
These are not a means to your salvation, but a reflection of your heart posture. The life of a disciple of Christ is a life of discipline, not discipline of rules and regulations, but true Biblical discipline that converts the soul and transforms the mind. Biblical faith is not frozen in formulas or frying in fanaticism, but it's walking in moderation with true discernment and godly wisdom. Faith is an action based upon a belief sustained by sure confidence. It's the action that cultivates a spirit to receive, learn, and listen, understanding that God's Word and God's ways reign supreme in His body of disciplined learners. Faith demands a response! The 5 Pillars of Faith are the basics for the disciplined Christian. They all hang on the greatest pillar of all: The just shall live by faith!

Pillar 1: First Day Living. Be consistent to give God the first day, if the first day is holy, the rest is also holy. Be consistent within your own heart why you come into the house of God. The answer must be: because of

God the Father, God the Son, God the Holy Spirit, the Word of God, and the man of God.

Pillar 2: First Fruit Giving. Be consistent in your giving, if the firstfruit is holy, the lump is also holy. Consistently bring your tithe into the storehouse where you've been fed. Honor the Lord with the firstfruits of all your increase. Always operate in a spirit of giving.

Pillar 3: Daily Bible Reading. Consistently be in God's Word daily. Relationships require time spent together. Consistently equip yourself with the full armor of God, it is your shield and defense. Consistently be transformed by the renewing of you mind. Always search the Scriptures for yourself, for in them you will find life.

Pillar 4: Scripture Memory. Be consistent to hide God's Word in your heart. Be consistent in setting time aside regularly to memorize Scripture. Consistently use the Scripture as your weapon to fight against the warfare in the mind. Always be ready to give a defense for the hope that is in you.

Pillar 5: Flee Idolatry. Consistently separate yourself from the things that separate you from God. Consistently flee the distractions, the deterrents, and the discouragers. Keep prayer and thanksgiving at the forefront of everyday. Consistently make no provision for the flesh, the lust of the eyes, or the pride of life.

Consistency Of King David
David enters the stage of history on the heels of Saul's disappointing acts of presumption, pride, and disobedience. David is first described as one who was skilled in playing music; a mighty man of valor, a man of war, prudent in speech, a handsome person, and the Lord was with him (1 Samuel 16:18).

1 Samuel 17 describes David's mighty defeat against Goliath, the nine foot nine inch Philistine giant. From that point forward, in every mission that Saul sent him on, David acted wisely and brought victory over Israel's enemies. King David consistently led the men out to battle and brought them back again. He had consistency in his victories, for he continued to act wisely in all that he did and the Lord was with him (1 Samuel 18:13-14).

The consistencies of King David led to the conquering of much land for the kingdom of God's people. Time and time again, when it was time to go to battle, David went out to the front lines. At first by the commands of an angry and jealous King Saul, and later by the straight-forward instructions of the Lord Himself. King David had another admirable consistency about his battlefront mentality. He routinely sought the Lord's direction regarding if he should go, how he should go, and when he should go. The common theme throughout King David's victorious living was, "So David inquired of the Lord..."

You'll find these words quoted in 1 Samuel 23:2, 23:4, 30:8; 2 Samuel 2:1, 5:19, 5:23, 21:1; 1 Chronicles 14:10 and 14:14, to name a few. Get the picture? Are you consistently inquiring of the Lord for direction for you business, or do you only seek Him when you think you might be in trouble? There are two simple reasons why you fail to ask... One: You do not trust or believe the promises found in the Word of God; Two: You do trust and believe the promises in the Word of God, therefore you do not ask.

Need an explanation... When you absolutely know God is well able to do something for you, do you sometimes not ask for His help because you'd rather have it your way? If you ask, He might deliver you out of something that your flesh would rather keep for itself. Things that make you go "hmm..."

What is the battlefront to which God has called you to march? Is it simply to walk by faith? Is it to lift up the name of Jesus over your business? Is it to build your business on Biblical principles? Is it to bring in the unrighteous manna for the kingdom of God? (Note: for the kingdom of God, not for your own self-seeking focus of temporal satisfaction.) Whatever the battlefront is for you, know one thing, when it's time to go to battle, that's exactly what you are expected to do! What happens if you don't hit the battlefield running when you are called? King David learned this answer first hand the hard way.

"It happened in the spring of the year, at the time when kings go out to battle, that David sent Joab and his servants with him, and all Israel; and they destroyed the people of Ammon and besieged Rabbah. But David remained at Jerusalem." -2 Samuel 11:1

This little inconsistency led to a consistent disaster. So it happens, during King David's battle absenteeism, he elicits a secret affair with Bathsheba, the wife of Uriah. She becomes pregnant. David tries to cover it up. That doesn't work; so he puts a contract kill on Uriah. David then loses the child and God let's him know the consequence of this stunt, "The sword will not depart from your house... and I will raise up adversity against you from your own house and I will take your wives before your eyes and give them to your neighbor, and he shall lie with your wives in the sight of this sun. For you did it secretly, but I will do this thing before all Israel, before the sun." (2 Samuel 12:11-12)

This is the moment of repentance when King David pens Psalm 51, "blot out my transgressions and create in me a clean heart!" God hears the sincerity of King David's heart and grants him his life and forgiveness, but his actions still came with a consequence. David pulls it back together, strengthens himself in the Lord and gets back on the battlefield (2 Samuel 12:26-31). Learn from David's example. There is a time for war and a time for peace. Be diligent to discern what season you are in and stay focused on the task at hand until you have the release to move forward into whatever that next season or task might be!

Consistency Of Joshua

It's interesting to see how God will use the consistencies, which people exercise in the early stages of their Christian walk to bring about His victories with His consistencies later in their walk.

Take Joshua for example, you first hear about Joshua in Exodus Chapter 17. He comes on the scene as one appointed by Moses to lead the Israelite men into battle against the Amalekites. Joshua did as Moses commanded and victory was had that day. Joshua soon becomes identified as Moses' assistant and one of his choice men. This is where it gets interesting. When God called Moses to ascend Mount Sinai to speak with him, it is written that Joshua also went. Now when the glory of the Lord appeared in the cloud, Moses went into the midst of the cloud on the mountaintop while Joshua awaited his return. Joshua seems to be forming the discipline of consistently waiting in faith for the direction of the Lord, by the hand of Moses.

Move forward a few chapters to Exodus 33, and you see the same tenacity as Joshua consistently stays at the door of the tabernacle. It seems an understatement to say that being in the presence of the glory of God was Joshua's heart posture. It is really a part of his whole being. This is the type of consistency that provides a gateway for God to do amazing things through ordinary men; or, more specifically, ordinary men with extraordinary faith and extraordinary love for the Lord.

"So the Lord spoke to Moses face to face, as a man speaks to his friend. And he would return to the camp, but his servant Joshua the son of Nun, a young man, did not depart from the tabernacle." -Exodus 33:11

Some forty years later, Joshua now has the task of leading the Israelites into the Promised Land. The opening scene in the book of Joshua retains Joshua's focus on the Lord. Joshua knows God is about to do something big and calls for the whole camp to consecrate themselves to the Lord. Follow his example; when you know God is about to do something big, circumcise your heart and separate yourself to Him. Let the presence of the Lord go before you and follow it! (i.e. the Jordan River crossing, Joshua chapters 1-5)

Joshua's earlier consistencies paved a way for God to consistently use him to drive out the enemy and bring about victories as the Israelites take over their promised land. First Sihon, then Og, then Jericho and eventually Ai. The five Amorite kings and the five Jerusalem kings were next to fall into the hands of Joshua and the children of Israel. God can and will use your consistency in the small things to bring about victories in the larger things. Amen!

Consistency Of God's Word
There is a consistency throughout God's Word that surpasses the intellectual mind of even the brightest of scholars. It is an amazing thing when you stop to consider how the Word of God was written and compiled during a period of over thousands of years by many different men in many different parts of the world. One thing is for sure, it was God breathed, God inspired and God authored by the same Holy Spirit working though the hands of faithful men. The consistency of God's character is also unbending, as Peter and Paul both put it, "God shows partiality to no one." (Acts 10:34 and Romans 2:11). He is the same yesterday, today and forever (Hebrews 13:8). And His Word endures forever (Psalm 119:160 and 1 Peter 1:25). All of His promises are faithful and true (2 Chronicles 1:20).

God's Promises

One of the hardest hurdles to cross when dealing with the consistency of God's promises is the time frame. To God, who operates outside of the dimension of time, one thousand years is as a day and one day is as one thousand years. To man, who is totally governed by time, impatience and doubt can easily set in, and that can quickly lead to inconsistency in his behavior. It doesn't take much for the enemy of worry, doubt and fear to take you off course and deteriorate your trust in God that He will keep His promises. Sadly, it is in the delay of God's promises, that you begin to second-guess yourself and God's Word. Did He really promise that? Is it really going to happen? Maybe I read into it.

The Scriptures give many accounts of God making commitments to His people and then allowing vast amounts of time to go by before completely fulfilling those commitments. This was no accidental delay, but it was intentional to build and test both patience and trust. However, to those who would faithfully wait on Him, He always made good on His Word.

How do you know that He will make his Word good today? You now have the more sure prophetic word confirmed: The Word of God! How blessed are those who have the full revelation of God's character and plan for His people right at their fingertips.

God has been consistent with His people since the Garden of Eden. Now if you will only be consistent in implementing the principles He's given you through His Word. You can rest assured based on the history you have in the Scriptures, that He will be consistent in working into all things and all your situations for His good and for His glory (Romans 8:28).

"Jesus Christ is the same yesterday, today and forever." -Hebrews 13:8

The 72 Hour Rule

This is among one of the single-most important principles requiring unwavering consistency in your company. In the law of measurement, there are three dimensions: length, width, and height. This is what makes up a solid. Accordingly, three speaks of solidity. It is a symbol of completeness or perfection. This is the same completeness suggested in the Triune Godhead of the Father, Son and Holy Spirit. It denotes Divine testimony or manifestation. This manifestation can be resurrected in things moral, physical, or spiritual.

Take for example Jonah. He was in the belly of the whale three days and three nights (seventy-two hours). It was after his repentant prayer and vow of thanksgiving that God spoke to the fish, and it vomited Jonah onto dry ground (Jonah 1:17-2:10). Jesus uses this same allegory as a sign of His resurrection in Matthew 12:40, "For as Jonah was three days and three nights in the belly of the great fish, so will the Son of Man be three days and three nights in the heart of the earth."

Christ was in the public ministry three years before the manifestation of His prophesied death and resurrection was revealed. The inscription over the cross, written in three different languages, testified to the completeness of His rejection by man. However on the third day, God manifested His glory in the resurrection of His Son Jesus Christ! Three is the symbol of Divine manifestation and Divine perfection.

"For as Jonah became a sign to the Ninevites, so also the Son of Man will be to this generation." -Luke 11:30

So, what does this three-day rule have to do with you and your business? Everything! It is God's standard timetable of revealing those things, which are hidden. Joshua learned this lesson the hard way. Joshua had marching orders from the Lord to take over the promised land of Canaan. When the men of Gibeon (a town nearby) heard how the Israelites were beginning to conquer the land, they worked craftily and pretended to be ambassadors from a faraway place.

Based on the outward appearance, their story appeared to be true, so Joshua and the Israelites made a covenant of peace with them. "Now then it happened at the end of three days and three nights, after they had made a covenant with them, that they heard that they were their neighbors who dwelt near them" (Joshua 9:16). According to custom, they are now stuck with them and their premature treaty.

Have you ever made a decision and then come to find out the next day, it was the opposite of what you meant to accomplish? Maybe you've bought something on a no return policy one day and found it half price the next day..... ughhhh! Maybe you've said, "Yes" to something that you now wish you would have said, "No" to.

Keep in mind, everything you need to know may not always be revealed in 72 hours. At times, God may require a more patient holding process from you. The general rule of thumb: Give any major decision 72 hours before making the final call or signing on the dotted line. Things can appear one way, when in actuality they are gravely different. Give it three days and let God manifest the truth!

1 2 3

Watch... Wait... Listen

PILLAR 5: FLEE IDLENESS

CHAPTER TWENTY:
Put Your Business In Gear!

The greatest idea, the perfect product, and even the perfect pitch are nothing if they are left running idle. To help establish this point, let's start with the basics of what it really means to run idle.

idle
(1) not active or in use; not working; lazy; characterized by inactivity. (2) without purpose or effect; pointless; without foundation; to move aimlessly.

Is this how you would describe yourself or your business? We hope not, but if so, don't expect a different result if you keep doing the same thing over and over again. You will still get nothing!

Interestingly enough, there are homophonic words at play here (words that sound the same but have different meanings). Not only must you avoid running idle, but you must also run from idols. An idol is any person, place, or thing that leads your time, talent, and treasure to itself and away from God. In the case of your business, it is the distractions, large or small, that keep you from running your business with a diligent purpose. Staying true to your mission statement and consistent with your written vision will aid you in this ongoing task.

Putting your business in gear involves the ability to use solid leadership skills, to surround yourself with dynamic team players, and to successfully manage and support your business operations. God's Word is packed full of admonitions for your understanding and directions for just such topics. Pillar 5: Flee Idleness, will unveil from the Scriptures some amazing examples of powerful men and women who knew the value of running from idols and, in like manner, knew how to avoid running idle. So now, if you are willing, He is well able to accomplish great things through you and your business!

"So shall My Word be that goes forth from My mouth; it shall not return to Me void, but it shall accomplish what I please, and it shall prosper in the thing for which I sent it." - Isaiah 55:11

"Being confident of this very thing, that He who has begun a good work in you will complete it until the day of Jesus Christ." -Philippians 1:6

Many times in relationships, in business, or simply in life in general, there are past experiences and circumstances that can cause you to run idle. Worry, doubt, and fear begin to grow and can soon turn into procrastination, taking even the ambitious into captivity by a spirit of laziness. This kind of idleness has the ability to put you into a self-preservation freeze that will stop you from moving forward in faith and hinder you from reaching the goals set before you.

To suppose that you will never come into a place of idleness is as unrealistic as saying you'll never sin again. Romans 3:23 says that, "All have sinned and fallen short of the glory of God." And at one point or another, all will deal with idleness. Rather than getting caught up in the idea of never becoming idle, let's look at what it takes to identify idleness and how to flee from it.

"Brethren, I do not count myself to have apprehended; but one thing I do, forgetting those things which are behind and reaching forward to those things which are ahead, I press toward the goal for the prize of the upward call of God in Christ Jesus." -Philippians 3:13-14

Idleness sets in when we begin to focus on things past rather than things present or things to come. Paul encouraged the believers in Philippi to no longer care for the mistakes of their past, but to eagerly and earnestly set themselves toward the goal before them. Focus on the destination of the journey in front of you, keeping your mind stayed on the end that is in view. What is the destination of the journey of your faith-based company? Is it to glorify God through your day-to-day activities, to lead others in a more accurate direction of the gospel of truth, or to bring in provision for the kingdom of God? Know what your goal is and press toward it!

The Christlike Mind

Idleness is not just the lack of activity. Look again at the previously noted definition. Idleness is also the result of operating without purpose or effect. Without a solid foundation, a specific goal, or a clear vision for your company, your work can quickly become pointless. Things may be getting done, but if they are done in a spirit of aimlessness, what truly have you accomplished?

How will your faith-based company affect the lives of others? The answer starts with what you hold in your mind. Paul's letter to the Philippian church lays out a beautiful picture of what the Christlike mind ought to look like...

"Fulfill my joy by being like-minded, having the same love, being of one accord, of one mind. Let nothing be done through selfish ambition or conceit, but in lowliness of mind let each esteem others better than himself. Let each of you look out not only for his own interests, but also for the interests of others. Let this mind be in you which was also in Christ Jesus, who, being in the form of God, did not consider it robbery to be equal with God, but made Himself of no reputation, taking the form of a bondservant, and coming in the likeness of men. And being found in appearance as a man, He humbled Himself and became obedient to the point of death, even the death of the cross. Therefore God also has highly exalted Him and given Him the name which is above every name, that at the name of Jesus every knee should bow, of those in heaven, and of those on earth, and of those under the earth, and that every tongue should confess that Jesus Christ is Lord, to the glory of God the Father." -Philippians 2:2-11

A Christ-centered mind focuses on the things of God more than the things of the world or the desires of the flesh. It's a business mind that says, "How can this company make a difference in the business arena today!" Its ambition is not generated by selfish motives but by the Spirit of God working through you. It is a business whose mind is stayed on Jesus and His will and His agenda... ultimately for His glory!

The Battle Is In The Mind

Faith (Greek: Pistis) is an action word! It requires a forward movement. Operating a faith-based company demands an action on your part. A successful business begins with writing the vision and making it plain on tablets (Habakkuk 2:2). Therefore, write the plan, confirm it in God's Word, apply the 72-hour rule, and take appropriate action! An idle mind and an idle business alike are the devil's playground. Avoid them both!

Identifying Idleness

There are two key things to look for when identifying idleness within yourself, within your staff members, and within your company in general. Be on the lookout for: (1) Lack of production (2) Lack of purpose.

The Stagnant Mind

When the mind becomes stagnant, the body soon will follow. The stagnant mind usually results in stagnant production! It is the idle and unrenewed mind that gives way to the fiery darts of the enemy's attacks. Understand the battle is in the mind! You do not wrestle against flesh and blood, but against principalities and powers. These so-called powers are the thoughts that enter your mind. They can enter through the ear gate, through the eye gate, or even out of mid-air. Have you ever thought something and said to yourself, "Where on earth did that thought come from?" Well, if it wasn't of God, then it was likely from His and your adversary the devil.

His fiery dart is the attack on the mind. If you don't extinguish it, it will become a house of fire in your own mind. When you give heed to the seemingly little thoughts that creep in, they will quickly turn into a stronghold when left unchecked. God's Word says that you are to take every thought captive to the obedience of Christ (2 Corinthians 10:5). This means to rebuke the misaligned thoughts to the plumb line of God's Word. You cannot fight a thought with a thought! Sure, there may be a nugget of truth to it, but has that nugget gotten exaggerated in your own mind? The victory lies in fighting the thought with the Word of God. Hence the importance of Scripture memory as laid out in Pillar 4: Disciplined Actions.

Action Without Purpose

People seem to be doing their jobs, but nothing seems to be advancing. Sound familiar? Don't be afraid to make mid-course corrections! Have you or your team lost sight of the ultimate goal at hand? Has changing the world become about how much money goes into your bank account? When you loose your consistency of purpose, other things will begin to depreciate with it. Maybe it's time to get back to the basics. What is the driving force behind your business?

Thought vs. Thought

You cannot fight a thought with a thought! In Matthew's account of when Jesus was tempted by Satan in the wilderness, the text clearly shows that Jesus did not rebuke Satan with a thought. He rebuked him by quoting God's Word in context. Check it out for yourself...

Matthew 4:4....
"It is written, 'Man Shall not live by bread alone, but by every word that proceeds from the mouth of God.'" -Deuteronomy 8:3

Matthew 4:7....
"It is written, 'You shall not tempt the Lord your God.' " -Deuteronomy 6:16

Matthew 4:10....
"It is written, 'You shall worship the Lord your God, and Him only shall you serve.' " -Deuteronomy 6:13 & 10:20

Regarding the above questions now is not the time to be idle about it. "For with the heart one believes unto righteousness, and with the mouth confession is made unto salvation." (Romans 10:10) Confession has a two-fold function. One: it means to give praise and thanksgiving. Two: it means to agree with and to declare openly. Neither one of these are obtained in a state of idleness. Agree with the nugget of truth in the accusation against you and move forward to either rebuke it by God's Word or proclaim God's promise over it for that particular situation. His Word plus your mouth, these are the weapons of warfare!

The victory lies in the Word of God. It is your weapon of warfare. Without it, you are like a soldier unarmed for battle. If you have resolved that God's Word is living and powerful, sharper than any two-edged sword and it is the same yesterday, today and forever, then what Paul wrote to the Ephesians regarding spiritual warfare almost some 2000 years ago still applies today! To fight the good fight of faith, you must put on the whole armor of God. It is His Word that enables you to stand against the wiles of the devil.

Get Dressed!

As a believer, you are called to gird your waist with the belt of truth, to put on the breastplate of righteousness, to prepare your feet with the gospel of peace; above all, you are to take up the helmet of salvation and the sword of the Spirit, which is the Word of God; praying always with all prayer and supplication in the Spirit, being watchful to this end with all perseverance and supplication for all the saints (Ephesians 6:10-18).

How do you literally put on this armor? By putting on the mind of Christ! How do you put on the mind of Christ? By Faith and by spending time in the Word of God! The Word became flesh and dwelt among us. Christ is the living Word! God says He lifts His Word above His very name. Does that mean something to you Mr. or Mrs. Entrepreneur? Everything you need is in His Word. Get dressed for work in His Word and stop showing up naked to the office. If you're not getting clothed in His Word each morning, it is no wonder Satan keeps eating you for lunch. It's time to grow up and be matured by His life giving, battle fighting, enemy crushing Word.

Yes, this may be a little offensive to some, but if the shoe fits wear it. Or, more importantly if it did fit, trade them in for a new pair, namely the sandals of peace would be a nice trade. The Word says that offenses must come. If you can't handle a harsh word here, how do you plan to stand firm in real life scenarios?

Strength comes from identifying your weaknesses. When it comes to battle, the area in which a soldier or his squad appears to be weak is the area in which they will train the hardest. This is no exception for the entrepreneur. Identify your weakness and allow God's Word to turn it into your strength.

CHAPTER TWENTY-ONE:
Successful Leadership

Success Begins With Leadership
In order to successfully lead, you must first be able to follow. Take, for example, the successful conquering of the Promised Land accomplished through Joshua after he obediently followed Moses; or how about the great exploits of King David who first humbly followed King Saul; or the double portion that was on Elisha's life only after he served the greatest of all prophets, Elijah. You can't leave out Ruth, who by faith, followed the footsteps of Naomi; or Timothy who faithfully followed the apostle Paul as unto the Lord. Every great leader was once a great follower!

Entrepreneurs are often natural leaders. They have an innate ability to seek out opportunities that often lead to great accomplishments regardless of the obstacles set before them. They will overcome objections and tarry through trials for the greater good of the task at hand. They will see their tasks through to completion, either by personal commitment or strategic delegation.

A successful leader will see the end before he's even begun! This type of visionary leadership allows the entrepreneur to approve, disapprove, or redirect his plans according to the bigger picture. When seeing the bigger picture and the burden that lies before you, it's important that you do first things first! First up, unburden your heart to God. An effective leader must also be a humble leader, acknowledging that he is not self-sufficient, but rather is dependent upon the One who alone is all sufficient. Cast all your cares on Him and let Him carry the burden! (1 Peter 5:7). Now that He has got the load, seek His will, execute His strategies, and move forward by faith.

The Leadership Of Nehemiah
One of the most excellent examples of a visionary leader is found in Nehemiah, the governor of Judah during the fifth century BC. Nehemiah

was a man of God, full of wisdom, patience, skill, and perseverance. He had a task set before him to rebuild the destroyed and broken down walls of Jerusalem. He sought out divine guidance each step of the way, and accomplished through the personal commitment of many people what no man or men had been able to do before. A task that should have taken years to complete was accomplished in just fifty-two days! The entire book of Nehemiah is full of amazing leadership details you can glean from. For now you'll be looking at Nehemiah's inspired plan for success as illustrated in chapter 2.

He Gathered Information: This is not the time for you tell everyone what you are up to, but simply gather enough details to create a workable plan before you jump into the unknown without a parachute.

He Formulated A Plan: To have a workable plan, it is not necessary to have all the information, but it is crucial to have the necessary information, and then conceptualize and formulate a wise plan from it. Do not make the mistake of hibernating in a stage of information gathering only, never willing to make any decision. For you may soon find out that the opportunity to make a good decision has long passed you by.

He Implemented The Vision: It was now time to overcome the apathy of the people with enthusiasm. Enthusiasm is aroused by an ideal, which takes the imagination by storm, and becomes a definite intelligible plan for carrying that ideal into practice. The most effective leaders are able to get others to do what they want them to do, and have them like doing it. How? By throwing down a challenge.

He Worked In Unity: Nehemiah understood the benefit that equal participation had on morale, "We can," "Come let us," "Together we will." His challenge to work together for a greater common goal inspired the people in a personal way.

He Kept Them Informed: Part of Nehemiah's ability to arouse the people to build the wall was by winning their confidence and their trust. Trust was earned through honest communication. He shared with the people the victories that were already won and the progress made by their fellow brethren. Knowing and understanding the impact of the seemingly small role you may play as a part of the whole picture is motivation to "keep on going."

Mastering The Secrets That Overcome Obstacles

To succeed at a task when there is no opposition requires skill, but it takes the tenacity of a great leader to succeed when the work is being opposed. It is difficult to tell what a person is really made of until his "cup gets bumped." What spills out is a reflection of what is inside. When Nehemiah's cup of opposition got bumped, it allowed for the manifestation of his faithful leadership to brilliantly shine through.

When your business begins to excel, the likelihood is that at some point you will run into opposition. During the rebuilding of the walls of Jerusalem, you find that their success brought some pretty specific forms of opposition, likely because: (1) Others are threatened. (2) Others are jealous. (3) Your agenda is different from their agenda. (4) Others feel excluded. (5) Others are suspicious of your motives. (6) Others feel they'll be humbled or lose face. (7) Others don't like change and prefer their traditions. (8) Others want to deliberately confuse you.

Throughout all of this opposition, Nehemiah continued to show the Christ-like quality of enduring strength. He remained submissive to God, having no other plan for his life than what God had for him. In the same way in which Christ was submissive to the Father during His great persecution.... "Not My will, but Thy will be done." (Matt 26:39). Nehemiah stayed focused on the goal at hand, not deviating even in the slightest degree from the task to which God had called him.

He exercised wisdom in handling the complex situations, realizing that not all problems will have the same answer; each is to be handled with God's wisdom and specific directions. Nehemiah had courage to act decisively, knowing that he served God and not man. God's purposes will always reign supreme. Nehemiah was not afraid to act boldly in the face of his enemies, nor his subordinates. He fought the good fight of faith and finished the race! (2 Timothy 4:7-8)

Christ said that they hated Him without a cause, and if they persecuted Him, they will persecute you. If they brought trouble to Nehemiah's building project, don't be surprised when you see opposition coming your way in your building project. Take it in stride; you're amongst good company; you obviously must be doing something right! Now it's time to put on your spiritual goggles and take a look at Nehemiah's troublemakers. Allow the Lord to lead you in what He would have you glean from these powerful passages from the book of Nehemiah.

Opposition Brings Ridicule: Aside from opposition being so easy to implement, it's demoralizing and frequently effective. It strikes at your hidden insecurities and weaknesses, and mocks the promises of God. Nehemiah's response: He takes it to God in prayer, then it's on with the building! Something similar to the old World War II slogan, "Praise the Lord and pass the ammunition!"

Opposition Brings The Threat Of Violence: This comes when you are at a low point, tired and bogged down from the inside out. This opposition didn't go away because Nehemiah prayed, but it increased and became more threatening. Fear brought discouragement to the team (Israel), but to the leader (Nehemiah), it brought hope, for he knew the strength of God and the limitations of the enemy. Nehemiah's response: He paused the work, armed the people, posted guards, protected the family, established procedures, and encouraged the team. Be confident that what the Lord has started, He will complete (Philippians 1:6).

Opposition Also Comes From Within: Just when you think you have overcome, the attacks from the inside are worse than those from the outside! It's sad, but often true, when you find that you have met the enemy and it is you! These are those who profess to be Christians, yet kill God's prophets, and it is still going on today. Wrong conduct existed among believers; by exploitation, the rich were still getting richer, and the poor were still getting poorer. You cannot work in one accord when strife is in your midst. Nehemiah's response: He paused the work, united the team, straightened things out through prayer and repentance, then went back to building. Get it right before you build the walls any higher.

Opposition Escalates To Personal Attack: This is a three-part attack by intrigue, innuendo and intimidation. Intrigue wants to suck you in and take you off course, especially when you're almost done with the task at hand. Avoid the temptations of repeated requests and desires to please others. Do not compromise the greater good for the lesser good. Stand firm and just say, "No!" Innuendo is the hardball, dirty trick attack through open letters (gossip and rumors). Reply by denying what is false and stating what is true. Intimidation is the messenger of fear brought by the false prophet for profit. If the message doesn't line up with God's Word, then it's not from God!

Welcome to the wonderful world of Christianity; whoever said it would be easy was lying. Even the Scriptures recognize this walk as a battle

- "Fight the good fight of faith" (1 Timothy 6:12). In like manner, it is also a race - "I have finished the race" (2 Timothy 4:7), and a sacrifice - "Present your bodies as a living sacrifice, holy, acceptable to God which is your reasonable service" (Romans 12:1).

Bible study takes work, prayer takes time, witnessing arouses persecution, and living a holy life in the midst of the temptations of this world is extremely difficult. Because of such difficulties, can you be excused from time to time to just do your own thing... maybe get a break from the blood sweat and tears? Jesus did not promise His followers a comfortable life, but a cross, one custom crafted for each individual. But understand, with the burden of that cross comes unsurpassable blessings. It is after times of great struggle that God brings about pleasant times of sweet rest. After warfare, there is victory, and after times of spiritual exertion, there are times of joyous celebration. This too, is in the story of Nehemiah. After great trial and tribulation, the walls were completed, the covenant was sealed, the walls and the people were dedicated, and a revival was at hand. At least until the next rebuke.... see the final chapter of Nehemiah.

The bottom-line, Nehemiah was able to succeed where others had failed, and God was glorified in the process. Let's recap some of those accomplishments. No doubt about it, his governorship of Judah begins with a triumphal entry:

(1) He secured permission to rebuild the walls of Jerusalem. (2) He developed a plan for constructing the walls. (3) He inspired a defeated and discouraged people to move in faith. (4) He overcame numerous and daunting oppositions, inside and out. (5) He completed the task at hand, namely the walls. (6) He encouraged and assisted in a nationwide revival. (7) He organized and repopulated the city with believers.

This is still merely a highlight from which you can glean from the book of Nehemiah. If you get the chance, study the gates of Nehemiah and how the succession of their existence has a unique parallel to the Christian walk. Another great resource worth checking out is the Expositional Commentary on Nehemiah by James Montgomery Boice, some nuggets of which have been highlighted here.

The Leadership Of Joshua
Joshua, son of Nun, assistant to Moses and commander of the military, which led the Israelites into the Promised Land, was a God-fearing man in

whom the Holy Spirit dwelt (Numbers 27:18). Joshua's leadership provides a model of faithful obedience to God's written Word and its relationship to conquering what is set before us in order to receive the promises that lie ahead. After the death of Moses, the Lord spoke to Joshua saying:

"Only be strong and very courageous, that you may observe to do according to all the law which Moses My servant commanded you; do not turn from it to the right hand or to the left, that you may prosper wherever you go. This Book of the Law shall not depart from your mouth, but you shall meditate in it day and night, that you may observe to do according to all that is written in it. For then you will make your way prosperous, and then you will have good success. Have I not commanded you? Be strong and of good courage; do not be afraid, nor be dismayed, for the Lord your God is with you wherever you go." - Joshua 1:7-9

These three verses are among the most powerful driving forces of Joshua's leadership campaign. Let's break it down a bit. For starters, in order to observe God's Word, you must know what It is. This means you must get in there and read It for yourself. Joshua was told not to just know It, but to talk about It. The Word of God was not to depart from his mouth wherever he went or whomever he was with. The Lord likewise commanded Joshua to meditate in It. This implies reasoning about It and deducing things from It, getting It into your mind where It becomes part of your day-to-day reasoning and thinking, and influences your way of life and your entire decision making process. Like Joshua, you are called to obey God's Word, according to the spirit of the law as it is written. Do not try to second guess or improve on God's instructions. Joshua sets the example that we do not need increasingly clever methods or clever people to succeed, but rather obedience that is informed and motivated by the living and abiding Word of God to make your way prosperous.

Even as a young man, Joshua knew and understood the value of God's presence. Exodus 33:11 says that he would not depart from the door of the tabernacle. Later we read in Joshua 5:13-15, when faced by the Commander of the Lord's army, Joshua learned that the importance isn't about whether God is on your side or not, but rather if you are on His side! Throughout the great exploits of Joshua, the Scriptures show that his heart did not depart from the Lord.

Keeping The Camp Clean

Joshua had the character and attitude essential for God-given victories. He understood the fatal result of pride and presumption, and he knew the difference between marching and keeping your mouth shut and shouting and proclaiming victory. Joshua also learned first-hand the lesson about the relevance of keeping the camp clean.

As a leader of your faith-based company, you are held to a higher standard of obedience than your counterpart associates in the world. What you may have gotten away with yesterday, God may chastise you for today. Just as God held Joshua accountable for Achan's sin, so also are you held responsible for the sin in your company. A little leaven leavens the whole lump, and a rotten apple still spoils the whole bunch. Keeping the camp clean requires discipline and discernment. Let's look at how Joshua handles this situation.

The sin of Achan is right on the heels of one of the greatest and most unique victories Israel had ever seen or experienced, the destruction of Jericho. Before the walls came tumbling down, Joshua made the rules and protocol very clear, "And you, by all means abstain from the accursed things, lest you become accursed when you take of the accursed things, and make the camp of Israel a curse, and trouble it." (Joshua 6:18)

Next up is Ai, but to the surprise of Joshua, Israel experiences defeat. "Why?" Joshua asks the Lord; because Israel has both stolen and deceived regarding the accursed things. Joshua now has the task of finding the offense and making things right before God. When Achan gets called out, he admits his guilt in stealing the Babylonian garment, the silver shekels, and the wedge of gold. It was Achan's own dissatisfaction with God's provision that led to his rebellion, which led to disobedience. Learn from Achan, coveting the outward appearance of worldliness, the materialism of this world, and keeping for yourself what belongs to the Lord will get you and your household stoned! Dissatisfaction and covetousness must be brought to death. It is a part of your flesh that doesn't want to die, but with the crucifixion of the flesh comes change, change that brings hope and hope that allows the mercies and grace of God to show through your life.

Is there defeat in your camp? Have you gone from idle to reverse? Maybe you need to check and see if Achan's sin is in your midst. Clean the camp or God will clean it for you! Higher levels equal higher devils, which equals higher responsibilities!

The Influence Of Esther

Oftentimes people treasure security way too much, even knowing that it carries no guarantees in this life. Possessions can be destroyed, beauty fades, relationships can be broken, and death is inevitable. The very perception of security is often the key reason that keeps individuals from going into business for themselves.... fear of the unknown paycheck! Real security, then, must be found beyond this life. Only when your security rests in Jesus and his unchanging nature can you face the challenges that life is sure to bring your way.

Esther's beauty and character won the heart of King Xerxes as he declared her to be his queen. But, even in her favored position, there was no security that her life wouldn't be in jeopardy for the actions she was about to take. Esther was in a place that required her to risk her life on behalf of her people. When Haman's plan to destroy the Jews became public, Mordecai (Esther's cousin and up-bringer) lamented and turned to Queen Esther to save the Jews by pleading with the King. He gives this message to Esther...

"Do not think in your heart that you will escape in the king's palace any more than all the other Jews. For if you remain completely silent at this time, relief and deliverance will arise for the Jews from another place, but you and your father's house will perish. Yet who knows whether you have come to the kingdom for such a time as this?" - Esther 4:13-14

Continuing in Chapter 4, Esther's response to Mordecai, "Go, gather all the Jews who are present in Shushan, and fast for me; neither eat nor drink for three days, night or day. My maids and I will fast likewise. And so I will go to the king, which is against the law; and if I perish, I perish!"

Esther's Faith Response

Was Esther afraid that the unpredictable nature of the king might have her justly executed for such an act, or would she rely on her faith that there is Someone greater and more powerful than the king who is in control? Although there was time for prayerful consideration, there was no time for idleness; her faith would demand a response! Understand the context here; if she doesn't do it, it won't get done! When Mordecai tells her deliverance will arise from another place, the literal translation is, "God will bring deliverance through a second direction." This doesn't mean by another person, it means He will choose another direction to get the attention and obedience of Esther. Friend, if you don't do what you are called to do, it won't get done the way you would have done it! It is possible someone else might do it, but not the same way God custom-crafted you for that specific task. Forget about the security of your self-preservation freeze and move forward by faith. This is why God so graciously admonishes you with His Word, so you can learn from the examples set before you.

How much of your security lies in your material possessions, your position, or even your reputation? God has not placed you in your present position for your own benefit. He has put you where you are to serve Him. As in Esther's case, this may involve risking your security at times (man's perception of security). Are you willing, like Esther, to let God be your ultimate security?

Esther: an orphan, despised minority, exiled captive, beauty queen, and trophy wife. Yet what defined Esther and gave her a place in history was the faithfulness and courage of her character, as shown in her actions. Her story is not only an example of the proper relationship of a godly woman to her husband, but also of children to their parents, and employees to their employers.

Orphaned (2:7): Without a mother or father, just like you before Christ adopted you as His own son or daughter.

Covered (2:7 &11): Under a spiritual and fatherly covering; wives to husbands, employees to employers, believers to Christ.

Beautiful (2:7-8): Her character was her attractiveness and her heart posture was her beauty. Her meekness was shown through her gentle and submissive behavior.

Obedient (2:10,12-14, 20-23, 4:14, 7:4): To her covering: concealing, delivering, and revealing just as she was told. Submitted to twelve months of special preparation, diet and disciplined behavior.

Unselfish (2:15): Took the advice of wise council rather than her own wants and desires.

Influential (3:8-11, 4:11b): The absence of your spiritual influence matters to your covering, husband, employer, Bible study leader, workout partner, etc.

Compassionate (4:4, 8:6): Distressed with her people; having the character trait of being empathetic and comprehensive to the state of others around you.

Encourager (4:4b): Comforted and provided Mordecai with a change of garments. Exchanged the spirit of heaviness for the garments of praise (Isaiah 61:3).

Researcher (4:5,11,12): Get all the facts before acting too quickly. If information is second-hand and contrary to what you know, take time to verify it.

Correctable (4:13-14): Be willing to accept rebuke, redirection, and correction from those who are over you. The Lord chastens the ones He loves.

Non-materialistic (14:2, 15-16 *NRSV): Came humbly before God without her splendid apparel but covered in ashes. She took no joy in her possessions, using them only when appropriate.

Genuine Joy (14:18 *NRSV): Wealth does not bring genuine joy, but knowledge and understanding from God does (Proverb 3:13, Job 28:28).

Courageous (4:16, 15:5-15 * NRSV): Do it afraid! When things seem terrifying in your sight, God can bring gentleness to the fiercest of situations (Daniel 6:22).

Proper Honor (5:1): When it's time to put on your royal robe, do it with honor; whether it's your spouse's favorite outfit, your Sunday best, or your uniform for work.

Directness (7:3-4, 6): Get to the point without wasting the king's (covering's) time with excessive words or unnecessary babble (Matt 6:7, Proverb 10:19).

Intuitiveness (7:4b): Pointed out what was of personal interest to her king rather than over emphasizing what was of interest to her (potential material losses).

Non-nagging (7:7-8): State your case, then shut your mouth, and let the Holy Spirit convict your covering as He sees fit.

Generous Giver (8:1-2): She appointed the blessings she just received to Mordecai for his keeping. Are you willing to give away what you just got? (Luke 6:38).

Communicator (9:29-32): When given the opportunity, a properly worded letter can effectively communicate and minister to many people.

Redeemed (2:7a & 17, 9:22): God turns orphans into queens, sorrow into joy, and mourning into dancing. What the enemy meant for evil, God meant for good!

Women In The Bible
The Bible is full of women who became unexpected heroines and surprising instruments of God's unique design in history. Though it is easy to overlook their significance, women played many crucial roles in Scripture. Sometimes what the Scriptures do not say about a person can be as powerful or as important as what they do say about someone.

Notable women are seen throughout the Scriptures navigating through life, as they know it using faith, discernment, and good judgment as their tools. Like yourself, they too are a mixture of strength and weakness, courage and fear, hope and despair, and dreams and disappointments. Their circumstances and struggles, along with their characters and victories, can teach you a great deal about coming out of a life of idleness and into a life of faith.

Deborah & Jael (Judges Chapters 4 & 5)
The Israelites are in the Promised Land, but are struggling through their ongoing cycles of Apostasy-Oppression-Repentance-Deliverance. Without a godly leader, "Everyone did what was right in his own eyes." Deborah is introduced in the Scriptures as both a prophetess and a judge, roles that seemed to be more exclusive to men at the time, however, she offered both prophecy and judgment to Barak when she communicated God's will to him. Despite Deborah's military directions to Barak, he would remain idle unless Deborah went with him to fight against Sisera. Her words were decisive, "I will surely go with you; nevertheless there will be no glory for you in the journey you are taking, for the Lord will sell Sisera into the hand of a woman."

The Lord fought for the people that day and overtook the enemies of Israel, but Sisera escaped and ran for safety to the camp of Heber the Kenite. To his surprise, rather than finding comfort from his ally's wife, he received a laced cup of milk and a tent peg through his head. Deborah's prophesy came to pass and Jael was God's instrument of deliverance. Even when people refuse God's orders, like Barak, His plans cannot be thwarted. To whom it may concern, man of God, if you don't step up, God may send a woman to do your job in your place. Ouch!

Naomi & Ruth (The Book Of Ruth)

This is a beautiful story of obedience and redemption. Naomi, having lost her husband and both her sons, found herself in bitter despair and without hope. She decided to leave her dwelling in Moab to return home to Bethlehem. She advised her two daughters-in-law to return to their homes. Orpah did so, but Ruth would not. She clung to Naomi saying, "For wherever you go, I will go; and wherever you lodge, I will lodge; your people shall be my people, and your God, my God." Ruth's willingness to abandon everything to follow God's ways is an example for all. Ruth's decision to follow Naomi puts a greater responsibility on her spiritual mother. Naomi must lead and advise Ruth with wise discernment in order to bring her to the feet of Boaz, her kinsman redeemer. The bottom-line: Naomi led, Orpah fled, Ruth obeyed, and Boaz redeemed.

Rahab (Joshua Ch. 2 & 6; Matthew 1:5; Hebrews 11:31; James 2:25)

Rahab is one of only two women mentioned in the Hall of Faith in Hebrews 11. The odds were against her as a harlot, a gentile, an Amorite, and a women who dwelt among unbelievers. Without a teacher and as a foreigner to the covenant, she did not possess the advantages or promises of the Jews. But, despite all this she believed without having seen God in action, and she anticipated God's promises without being part of God's own people. Her hearing went past her ears and into her heart as she believed by faith. Her loyalty was no longer to her people or their corrupt city, but to a faith that was growing in the Lord. Rahab married Salmon, from the tribe of Judah, gave birth to Obed, who begot Jesse, who begot King David, whose lineage led to Christ.

Rahab was anything but idle and she had many qualities worth mimicking: she was hospitable and kind-hearted, a multi-tasker, laboring with flax on her roof top (used for making cloth), a risk taker, unselfishly willing to protect her family, obediently able to keep silent, gentle as a dove and wise as a serpent, and she was the foolish thing that God used to confound the wise. Rahab lived in a world of corruption, yet heard and believed and laid down her life to identify with God's chosen remnant, placing her hope (tiqvah) in Christ... Oh to be like Rahab!

Martha & Mary (Luke 10:38-42; John 11:1-3, 17-45, 12:1-8)
Martha and Mary were sisters of Lazarus and close friends of Jesus. Their characters portray both ends of the Christian spectrum, realizing that you cannot be so spiritually minded that you are no earthy good, nor so caught up in good works that you have no spiritual value. Martha is the one you find busy serving in the kitchen while her sister Mary sits at the feet of Jesus listening to His teachings. In frustration of Mary's lack of help, Martha asks Jesus to intervene. To the surprise of Martha, Jesus answers her, "Martha, Martha, you are worried and troubled about many things. But one thing is needed, and Mary has chosen that good part, which will not be taken away from her." Again later we see Martha serving dinner and attending to guests while Mary anoints the feet of Jesus with costly oil and wipes them with her hair.

One has a willing heart to serve while the other desires a place of intimacy. The choice is then not between Martha or Mary, for both are required and necessary, "Love the Lord your God with all your heart...and your neighbor as yourself." (Mark 12:30-31). Mary has chosen the better part, but the works of Martha are still necessary. Can you relate to having the proper balance in your work place?

The Virtuous Wife (Proverbs 31:10-31)
These are the words of King Lemuel's mother as she taught him. One commentator, James Vernon McGee, suggests that Lemuel was another name for Solomon, further suggesting that these words of advice would then be from his mother Bathsheba... an interesting thought! Let's take a closer look at this virtuous woman as described in the Scriptures.

"Who can find a virtuous wife? For her worth is far above rubies. The heart of her husband safely trusts her; so he will have no lack of gain. She does him good and not evil all the days of her life. She seeks wool and flax, and willingly works with her hands. She is like the merchant ships, she brings her food from afar. She also rises while it is yet night, and provides food for her household, and a portion for her maidservants. She considers a field and buys it; from her profits she plants a vineyard."

"She girds herself with strength, and strengthens her arms. She perceives that her merchandise is good, and her lamp does not go out by night. She stretches out her hands to the distaff, and her hand holds the spindle. She extends her hand to the poor, yes, she reaches out her hands to the needy. She is not afraid of snow for her household, for all her household is clothed with scarlet. She makes tapestry for herself; her clothing is fine linen and purple."

"Her husband is known in the gates, when he sits among the elders of the land. She makes linen garments and sells them, and supplies sashes for the merchants. Strength and honor are her clothing; she shall rejoice in time to come. She opens her mouth with wisdom, and on her tongue is the law of kindness. She watches over the ways of her household, and does not eat the bread of idleness. Her children rise up and call her blessed; her husband also, and he praises her: 'Many daughters have done well, but you excel them all.' Charm is deceitful and beauty is passing, but a woman who fears the Lord, she shall be praised. Give her of the fruit of her hands, and let her own works praise her in the gates."

The Virtuous Woman
It is important to understand that this virtuous woman is not some unreachable goal of perfect womanhood to be obtained, but it is a promise that has been made. Like all the promises in God's Word, this, too, is a promise available and claimable to those who earnestly seek His will.

An Excellent Wife
Compare this to the wife in Proverbs 12:4, "An excellent wife is the crown of her husband, but she who causes shame is rottenness to his bones." In this case, the virtuous or powerful woman of noble character is contrasted with the woman who is disgraceful or causing shame. The acts of such a woman will eat away at her husband's strength and destroy his happiness.

The Crown Of Her Husband
The crown relates to wisdom and encircles the head (Proverbs 4:8-9). Wisdom, in effect, surrounds and protects the mind and brings honor to the head of the one who has it. This verse declares that the godly woman is also a crown to her husband. When she is received as God's gift, her husband will benefit from God's wisdom through her, much as Abraham did from Sarah (Genesis 21:12). The husband of such a woman will be "known in the gates;" he will be spoken of highly among his elders and peers. The woman who cultivates her relationship with God first, then relates appropriately to her husband, will powerfully influence him in every area of his life.

The Covered Wife

It's important to understand what is meant by, "Wife" in the context of these verses. To be husbanded means to be covered. A woman of virtue is covered and led by a husband, whether that is a spouse, a spiritual father, an overseer at work or, most importantly, Christ Himself. Her actions and attitude are submitted to and covered by another. Titus 2:4-5 again admonishes these godly women, "To love their husbands, love their children, to be discreet, chaste, homemakers, good, obedient to their own husbands, that the Word of God may not be blasphemed."

Proverbs 22:6, "She is to train up her children in the way that they should go, and when they are old they will not depart from it." This is the same ethical standard for training up individuals, sons and daughters in the faith, within your business. If or when the time comes that God should move them on, have you laid a foundation solid enough that wherever they go, they should not depart from the faith?

God has so much more to say about women in His design and the role they play in history, as well as in the future. However for this page, our time is short and our space is limited. Perhaps this might be a topic in itself for further curriculum to come... stay tuned.

Faith Couples: Abraham & Sarah (Genesis 11:27-25:9; Acts 7:2-5; Romans 4:2-3; Hebrews 11:8-22; James 2:23; 1 Peter 3:1-6)

They might not have a trophy in New York's Hall of Fame or a star on Hollywood's sidewalk, but in God's book, their Christlike faith entered them into God's Hall of Faith (Hebrews notable Chapter 11). Not only was Abraham the father of the Hebrew nation, but he was also considered the father of faith. As mentioned many times over, faith is acting upon a belief that is sustained by confidence. It is about believing, trusting, and acting upon something before you see the manifestation of that thing come to pass. This is exactly what Abraham did when God called him to get out of his fathers house and go to a land he did not know.

"Now the Lord had said to Abram: 'Get out of your country, from your family and from your father's house, to a land that I will show you. I will make you a great nation; I will bless you and make your name great; and you shall be a blessing. I will bless those who bless you, and I will curse him who curses you; and in you all the families of the earth shall be blessed.' So Abram departed as the Lord had spoken to him..." -Genesis 12:1-4a

---

Abraham and his wife Sarah were acting upon a promise before they saw the manifestation of that promise. By faith, they left the familiar without looking back and headed for a land they did not know. Abraham believed that which was spoken by the Lord and accepted it as true and trustworthy. In like manner, Sarah followed her husband as unto the Lord. Oh, if they only had a clue as to what was in store for them between the hearing of the promise and the ultimate receiving of the promise.

As a couple, Abraham and Sarah went through many trials and tribulations. More than once their marriage was on the brink of disaster. There was the time when Pharaoh tried to take Sarah as his wife, and then later the same thing happened with Abimelech of Gerar. In both cases, God restored Sarah back to Abraham with restitution. Then there was the drama and strife that surrounded that fleshly decision of theirs when Abraham had relations with Sarah's maidservant, Hagar, in order to produce a son (Sarah's hair-brained idea, by the way). Or, how about the continual scoffing and mocking they put up with between the son of the flesh, Ishmael, and the son of the promise, Isaac. This worked on Sarah's nerves for many years before she finally said to Abraham, "The bondwoman and her son must go!" Where strife exists, peace is at bay.

Sarah had influence in her relationship with Abraham throughout the years, but it is at this point where you can now see the mature nature of her influence. After years of maturity and experience, she has come to the conclusion that decisions made in the flesh must be sustained by the flesh. Sustaining the decisions made in the flesh is no easy task! It will rob you of your time, your talent, your treasure and quite possibly your sanity. Move on, cut the ties, and accept your losses!

There was a great promise on the lives of this famous couple. There were many things they had to endure together before they would see the light at the end of the tunnel. But, in spite of these trials, the Scriptures say that, by faith, they inherited the promise. The same promise that was placed on Abraham and Sarah some four thousand years ago is still alive and well today. It rests on the shoulders of faithful men and women who are not afraid to forsake all to follow Him! If God has placed this specific promise before you and your spouse, recognize what He is asking of you and step out into the unknown.

"By faith Abraham obeyed when he was called to go out to the place which he would receive as an inheritance. And he went out, not knowing where he was going. By faith he dwelt in the land of promise as in a foreign country, dwelling in tents with Isaac and Jacob, the heirs with him of the same promise; for he waited for the city which has foundations, whose builder and maker is God."

"By faith Sarah herself also received strength to conceive seed, and she bore a child when she was past the age, because she judged Him faithful who had promised. Therefore from one man, and him as good as dead, were born as many as the stars of the sky in multitude - innumerable as the sand which is by the seashore." - Hebrews 11:8-12

Faith Couples: Aquila & Priscilla (Acts 18:1-3, 24-26; Romans 16:3-4; 1 Corinthians 16:19)

Another faith couple worthy to be mentioned is Aquila and Priscilla. This couple comes on the scene of Scripture when the apostle Paul stayed with them during his travels to Corinth. The Scriptures say that Aquila and Priscilla were Jews who had recently come from Rome, which can lead to some interesting speculation. Earlier in Acts Chapter 2, on the Day of Pentecost, it says there were men from every nation, specifically including those from Rome, who were dwelling in Jerusalem. When there came a sound from heaven, as a rushing mighty wind, the multitude gathered together to see what the stir was all about. Could Aquila and Priscilla have been among the crowd? Maybe, or maybe not. Either way, they must have had some form of the truth instilled in them. For when they met Paul, they received him with readiness as he stayed with them in their personal home for some time.

Like Paul, Aquila and Priscilla were tent makers by trade. They were hard working business owners; entrepreneurs just like you. What makes them special is not what they did for a living, but rather what they did while they were earning a living. Tent making was simply the vehicle God had given them to produce an income. It is what they did with that income that made the difference. Based on the Scriptures, we can gather that it certainly must have helped support their travel expenses as they followed Paul from Corinth to Ephesus before returning to their home in Rome.

Living under the same roof, Aquila and Priscilla had a unique opportunity to spend quality time with the apostle Paul. They were able to hear the accurate teachings of Jesus and the power of His death and resurrection. They were instructed in the ways of God and in the baptism of the Holy Spirit and were able to teach others concerning the Truth. While they were in Corinth they came across a man by the name of Apollos...

"Now a certain Jew named Apollos, born at Alexandria, an eloquent man and mighty in the Scriptures, came to Ephesus. This man had been instructed in the way of the Lord; and being fervent in spirit, he spoke and taught accurately the things of the Lord, though he knew only the baptism of John. So he began to speak boldly in the synagogue. When Aquila and Priscilla heard him, they took him aside and explained to him the way of God more accurately." -Acts 18:24-26

Aquila and Priscilla had a special call on their lives as a couple of faith. They were leaders in the business arena, leaders in the community, and leaders in the church. Their most important task: To teach the way of God more accurately, including the baptism of the Holy Spirit!

Consider the change that Apollos made in his preaching after hearing the truth as told to him by Aquila and Priscilla. Acts 18:27-28 tells us that when Apollos arrived in Achaia, "He greatly helped those who had believed through grace; for he vigorously refuted the Jews publicly, showing from the Scriptures that Jesus is the Christ." There was a shift in what Apollos taught that reflected the Truth more accurately. If you haven't received the whole truth, it's hard to know if you're off course or not.

As a married couple, if you have an Aquila and Priscilla anointing on your life, then you ought to be asking yourself what kind of fruit is developing in those around you on whom you have an influence. Are you using the gifts God has given you to further the gospel of Christ, or is this just about making tents for yourself? Realize making tents is a crucial part of how you capitalize on the opportunity to talk to others. If you live in the United States, it is still a free country. Allow your business to be your ministry while you still can!

Being a leader takes courage, both as an individual and as a couple. Hold one another accountable to the vision statement and core principles of your faith-based company. Remind one another continually of the promises found in God's Word regarding your circumstance or situation. Two are greater than one and a threefold cord is not easily broken: you, your spouse and Christ Himself tying it all together (Ecclesiastes 4:12).

The Leadership Of King David
King David: shepherd, warrior, musician, poet, faithful friend, empire builder, sinner, saint, redeemer, failed father, adulterer, murderer, triumphant king, and a man after God's own heart! David is mentioned more than any other man in Scripture, second only to Christ Himself. There are countless lessons to be learned from the life of King David. He did so many things wrong, yet, at the same time, he did so many things right. He's the one man that most people can relate to; he's not an image of man's perfection, but an image of God's perfect choice.

The servants of Saul described David as one who is skillful in playing music; a mighty man of valor, a man of war, prudent in speech, a handsome person, and the Lord was with him. (1 Samuel 16:18) All of these are desirable traits not only for a king, but also for today's business leader.

The Bible makes no effort to hide David's failures, yet he is still remembered and respected for having a heart after God. Knowing how much you might relate to and share in David's failures, you should be curious to find out what made God refer to David as, "A man after My own heart" (Acts 13:22). David, more than anything else, had an unchangeable belief in the faithful and forgiving nature of God. He was a man who lived with great zeal. He sinned, but his conscience was quick to convict him. His confessions were from the heart, and his repentance was genuine.

Psalm 25 is a fantastic example of King David's transparent and humble heart posture. This Psalm reveals the distress David was feeling while his enemies seemingly triumphed over him. Even in the face of the seemingly impossible, David believed God for the miraculous. This is the same faith that God is looking for in you! A faith that is willing to trust that God will bring triumph out of tragedy. When tragedy strikes, tears often follow. It is important that you learn how to identify your tears when they come, for not all tears are the same.

The Scriptures identify eight kinds of tears: (1) Tears of sorrow and tragedy. (2) Tears of joy and dancing. (3) Tears of compassion. (4) Tears of desperation. (5) Tears of travailing. (6) Tears of Godly repentance. (7) Tears of demonic unbelief. (8) Tears of manly sorrow.

The tears that David wept before the Lord were tears of brokenness from spiritual warfare. Weeping may endure for a night, but joy comes in the morning (Psalm 30:5). As you pass through the "Valley of Weeping" rejoice, for your tears are filling a pool of blessing to swim in (Psalm 84:6). You may be crying now, but you'll be swimming in the blessings later (Psalm 125:6). The Lord desires such tears from a broken spirit and contrite heart.

Have you considered that the same heart posture, which was in King David, might be the missing link, which you need in order to have God's unmerited favor upon your business? King David knew he needed a Commander-In-Chief who was greater than himself. You also must know that you need a commander-in-chief over your faith-based company to truly appreciate that you have the Commander-In-Chief over your company!

Recovering After A Loss
When David was on the run from King Saul, there was a period of time when he dwelt in Ziklag (Philistine territory). It happened one day while David and his men were away, the Amalekites set fire to their camp and took captive all the women and children. It is in this setting that you can learn how David faced adversity and the steps he took to recover. The details of this event are told in 1 Samuel 30:1-31. It would be in your best interest to pause here and read that chapter in the Bible for yourself before moving on.

Done reading? Now, let's break it down into simple terms that we can relate to. In a nutshell, here are the eight key points that David displayed on his road to recovery after such a great loss...

1.   David lifted up his voice and wept - vs. 4

2.   David strengthened himself in the Lord - vs. 6

3.   David inquired of the Lord for direction - vs. 8

4.   David pursued with 400 men at his side - vs. 10

5. David attacked his enemy - vs. 17

6. David recovered all according to God's Word - vs. 18-19

7. David shared with those who stayed at camp - vs. 23-24

8. David made a statute and an ordinance - vs. 25-31

Do you realize what that ordinance entailed? It simply meant to share in the booty! In today's business arena it would be considered profit sharing. King David declared, "As his part is who goes down to the battle, so shall his part be who stays by the supplies; they shall share alike." (1 Samuel 30:24). When God opened our eyes to this truth, it was a profound revelation for our faith-based company (The Master's Touch). According to God's Word and our personal conviction, there is a relative dollar amount that is shared with every member of our staff according to the sales generated within the company, or shall we say, "booty collected." Praise God for the examples of the leaders that were set before us!

If you have recovered all that the enemy has stolen from you, be careful not to stop up God's blessing... but share it with others; and most certainly give God all the glory!

Many hidden truths about King David and his great exploits have been revealed throughout the David's 400 curriculum. His character has proven to be one of the central themes worthy of attention. Let's look at another of the more obscure passages. King David understood the value of having choice men around him. What began in the cave of Adullam as four hundred men who were in distress, in debt, and discontented has developed into an arsenal of strategic confidants. You can get a clearer picture of these characters by digging deeper into the history and meaning behind each of these men and their names.

"So David reigned over all Israel; and David administered judgment and justice to all his people. Joab the son of Zeruiah was over the army; Jehoshaphat the son of Ahilud was recorder; Zadok the son of Ahitub and Ahimelech the son of Abiathar were the priests; Seraiah was the scribe; Benaiah the son of Jehoiada was over both the Cherethites and the Pelethites; and David's sons were chief ministers." - 2 Samuel 8:15-18

Joab: The commander of the army - These are the ones trained and equipped for the battle of spiritual warfare.

Jehoshaphat: The recorder or the one who is to mark something to be remembered - These are the ones diligent in Scripture memory who have a special ability to recall what is written.

Zadok & Ahimmelech: The priests - These are those who are set apart and anointed to teach God's instructions through His Word. They serve as representatives of the people.

Seraiah: The scribe, one who is made aware of and concerned about the details - These are the ones to whom you delegate the details and they will see the job through to completion.

Benaiah: The commander of the guard - These are the ones who look after the welfare of the king and the succession of his kingdom.

Cherethites & Pelethites: The executioners & runners - These are the ones who bring correction and are appointed special messengers of the king's requests.

David's Sons: The chief ministers - These are the ones you keep closest to you.

With that said, it's fair to say, placing the right personnel around you with the natural gifts God has given them is not only wise, but it's absolutely crucial!

CHAPTER TWENTY-TWO:
Building Your Team

Dynamic Team Players

Building your team begins with surrounding yourself with competent people; people that can do the job at hand and do it well. Know your strengths and your weaknesses, and then place people around you who are strong in these areas. Don't be intimidated to hire someone who does a better job at something than you do... after all, isn't that the point of good help. Even Christ knew this principle, for He said that His followers would do even greater things than He. Keep in mind, no servant is greater than his master, but yet he has the ability to accomplish greater (or more) things. Remember back to the great leaders who were first great followers?

There is a distinct difference between God-given gifts (natural talents) and enjoyable interests. Placing people in an area where they are truly gifted will be one of your biggest assets. Consider applying the following principle when placing people and building teams within your business and workplace.

One: Expose The Gift. The gift must be exposed, likely God's doing and not your own. This is when the skills and natural talents that a person possesses become known and evident.

Two: Identify The Gift. You must identify the gift: Determine how this person's talent can best be utilized and uniquely custom fit into your organization.

Three: Place The Gift. You now have the responsibility to place the gift: A person placed in the area where God has specifically gifted him will empower him to do his job exceedingly well with a natural ease.

Lastly, don't be afraid to make mid-course corrections. Building a team takes time and patience; your first pick may not always be your perfect pick. So be prepared to adjust and shift as gifts become exposed, identified and placed.

Identifying The Gifts
It's one thing to identify the things you like to do, but it is another thing to identify what you are gifted to do. It's the uncommon thing that comes naturally to you. Before we go into further detail about placing gifted team players around you, we're going to take a side bar and go over what these gifts actually are and where they come from.

"Every good and perfect gift is from above, and comes down from the Father of lights. A man can receive nothing unless it has been given to him from heaven." - James 1:17 & John 3:27

Each spiritual gift contains unique qualities and special functions to fulfill the calling and purpose, which God has designed for our lives. The gifts of the Father contain basic life principles and core motivations. When combined with faith, they are what propel and drive us from point A to point B. These gifts were initially given to us individually, as He saw fit, and are part of our character traits.

Gifts From The Father
Let's take a closer look at some of the gifts listed in the Scriptures. We'll start with the seven gifts from the Father noted by the apostle Paul in Romans 12:3-8.

"For I say, through the grace given to me, to everyone who is among you, not to think of himself more highly than he ought to think, but to think soberly, as God has dealt to each one a measure of faith. For as we have many members in one body, but all the members do not have the same function, so we, being many, are one body in Christ, and individually members of one another. Having then gifts differing according to the grace that is given to us, let us use them: if prophecy, let us prophesy in proportion to our faith; or ministry, let us use it in our ministering; he who teaches, in teaching; he who exhorts, in exhortation; he who gives, with liberality; he who leads, with diligence; he who shows mercy, with cheerfulness."

Prophecy: To articulate and proclaim truth as in the Word of God; to speak forthrightness and insight when enabled by the Spirit of God. The prophetic gift enables individuals to project with accuracy events and numbers relative to upcoming situations. This gift is likely to be found in the entrepreneur, upper-management, chief financial officers and CPA's.

Ministry: To minister and render loving care or general service to meet the needs of others. This gift is likely to be found in nurses, doctors, dentists, those in the hospitality and hotel industry, bed and breakfast owners, chefs and catering specialists.

Teaching: The supernatural ability to explain and apply the truths received from God; the ability to make God's Truth clear to believers through diligent study and the enabling of the Holy Spirit. This gift is likely to be found in school teachers, vocational instructors, industry specialists, business coaches, personal fitness trainers, sporting event coaches, and music or vocal instructors.

Exhortation: To build up others with praise, provide encouragement, comfort and instruct with gentleness. This gift is likely found in middle-management positions, counselors, coaches, and teachers. You can quickly recognize this gift by its "cheerleader" type of personality.

Giving: To give hilariously with a spirit of generosity; to give to others when they are in need; giving of your time, talents or treasures. The true gift of giving is to be exercised without pride. This is likely to be found in non-profit leaders or a true public or community servant.

Leadership: The ability to guide, direct, and model as a godly example; to supervise or oversee as inspired by the Holy Spirit; to contribute in the developing of the body of Christ. This gift is to be exercised with diligence and care. This gift is likely to be found in a hospital's chief of staff, pastors, CEO's, school principals, team coaches, and most self-employed business owners.

Mercy: To relate to others in empathy, compassion, respect and honesty; to feel genuine sympathy with the misery of others, being compassionate to their state or circumstances. This gift is only effective when exercised with kindness and cheerfulness, and not out of guilt. This gift is likely found in the home health care specialists, and physical rehabilitation therapists.

Gifts From The Son

Christ has called, chosen, and anointed some as His elect domata. The word "domata" is of Greek origin meaning: to give, to grant, or to furnish something to someone. These unique gifts are for the facilitation and equipping of the body of Christ. Such leaders are called to prepare, train, make fit, or make qualified for service through the gift they have been given by Christ to edify the rest of the body as they come to the full understanding of the knowledge of God.

"And He Himself gave some to be apostles, some prophets, some evangelists, and some pastors and teachers, for the equipping of the saints for the work of ministry, for the edifying of the body of Christ." - Ephesians 4:11-12

Apostle: A special messenger or spokesperson of God, an overseer, one sent forth with orders; an advocate or supporter of a particular cause.

Prophet: A spiritually mature spokesperson or proclaimer with a special, divinely focused message from God to a person, the church, or the world. A person uniquely gifted at times with insight into future events.

Evangelist: To preach, testify, or witness in a way that brings unbelievers into the salvation of Jesus Christ, vital for the growing of the body of Christ in today's church.

Pastor: One who shepherds, nurtures, protects, and cares for the spiritual needs of the church body as individuals and as a whole. One specifically enabled to lead and guide others.

Teacher: One with the unique ability to teach others and communicate with wisdom and understanding the Word of God and the truths held within It.

The five-fold ministry defined above is found among the true shepherds leading the church body today. These special gifts are not exclusive, nor are they confined to a church building. Such gifts thrive in the leadership of true faith-based company owners. Christ has specifically elected pastors with these gifts to lead His church body. He likewise has elected special men and women in the business arena with some of these gifts to lead and instruct His people according to His ways and according to His purposes.

Gifts From The Holy Spirit
These gifts serve the purpose of profiting the body of the church or the entity of the faith-based company. These gifts are beneficial not only for the individual but especially for the church or organization as a whole in growing spiritually, and becoming strong in Christ.

"But the manifestation of the Spirit is given to each one for the profit of all: for to one is given the word of wisdom through the Spirit, to another the word of knowledge through the same Spirit, to another faith by the same Spirit, to another gifts of healings by the same Spirit, to another the working of miracles, to another prophecy, to another discerning of spirits, to another different kinds of tongues, to another the interpretation of tongues. But one and the same Spirit works all these things, distributing to each one individually as He wills.... And God has appointed these in the church: first apostles, second prophets, third teachers, after that miracles, then gifts of healings, helps, administrations, varieties of tongues." - 1 Corinthians 12:7-10 & 28

Applying Your Gifts In The Business Arena
Let's bring some clarity to this topic by placing these spiritual gifts in real life scenarios. To paint the best picture, we'll use a true story that occurred within our establishment. Names have been changed to preserve identities.

Wanting to increase the company's sales volume, we sought out to acquire an experienced Sales Manager, so we hired Henry for the position. He was doing a great job communicating with the sales staff over the last nine months and everyone truly loved him, however business had not shown any increase. As it turns out, Henry may have had years of sales-managing experience in other corporations, but his gifts were in helps, exhortation, and hospitality. These are great qualities for our client hospitality and event-coordination department, but not ideal for the sales department. Now, as a staff change was soon at hand, we discovered that John, another staff member, was showing his qualities in leadership through accurate administration and prophetic projections. His gift of foresight, teaching, and natural leadership was a more suitable fit for our Sales Manager position.

The Lesson From This Story... Experience isn't always your best fit! Identifying and placing yourself and others in the area where God has uniquely gifted you or them will always win out over experience in the end.

Remember, just because you've always done something, doesn't mean that's what you're called to do.

Surround Yourself Wisely

Surrounding yourself with competent people is more than just having wise men and women in your presence; it is about listening to and heeding godly counsel. You'll know the advice is wise when you can confirm it in God's Word. So what determines the competent from the incompetent? For the answer, you will need to read the opening scene of King Rehoboam's reign in 1 Kings 12:3-19. If you get lazy and don't pull out your Bible right now, the next part won't make as much sense.

Who Will You Listen To?

Rehoboam had a choice to receive counsel from the experienced elders who served his father well or from the young prideful peers he grew up with. Peer pressure can play a lasting role on our future, in this case, a not so favorable role. Just as misery loves company, so does rebellion love others to come into agreement with itself. Do you suppose things may have played out differently had Rehoboam listened to the competent men God had placed around him? Or, was his heart already bent toward the advice of his peers before he even asked?

"For by wise counsel you will wage your own war, and in a multitude of counselors there is safety." -Proverbs 24:6

Consider carefully who you seek counsel from. This applies both personally and professionally. If you know "Brother Bob" or "Sister Sally" will encourage and agree with you no matter what you say, stop and think for a moment... is this really the counsel you need? If you want a cheerleader when you're feeling down, so be it. But understand wise counsel is not born out of a spirit of flattery and divination; on the contrary, it becomes a hindrance, full of hypocrisy.

Christ speaks against such so-called friends in Matthew 15:7-9 saying, "Hypocrites! Well did Isaiah prophesy about you, saying: 'These people draw near to Me with their mouth, and honor Me with their lips, but their heart is far from Me. And in vain they worship Me, teaching as doctrines the commandments of men.'" Choose wisely whom you surround yourself with.

Finding The Best Fit

Take your time to find the right people for the right job. Not all people work well for all positions. Hiring a social butterfly probably is not in the best interest of your accounting department if you want to get things done quickly, however, a detailed math-junky would be great. Likewise, that same social butterfly won't survive in a boxed-in cubicle or dark computer room. They need interaction with people to flourish. Put them in customer service or sales where their natural communication skills can work as an asset to your establishment, rather than a detriment.

Keep in mind; it's helpful to identify the difference between a temporary behavior and an embedded personality or character trait. Behaviors can usually be adjusted, altered or improved, but embedded personality traits are part of who people are. They may be refined, but they won't disappear entirely.

Determining what people are made of is more than just identifying their personality traits and skill sets. It involves knowing what different individuals can handle and when and where they function at their best. It goes beyond identifying their own natural strengths and identifying the strength of Christ in them. Consider those who are like a rock, who can handle a great deal of pressure without cracking, and place them at the front of the battle-line (they can handle it). Or those who are easy-going with great flexibility who can perform just about any task at hand; placing them in supporting positions is a great fit.

Remember, this identification process applies not only to your staff, but also to you, the entrepreneur. Identifying your own weaknesses will aid you in knowing what to look for in others during the hiring process. Don't be afraid to hire someone who has more skill than you. The purpose of good help is to get help in areas where you need it most.

Despite all things being different, there must also be a common ground. Surround yourself with those who share in the vision of your company! Someone may have the right skills, but if in their heart they completely oppose what you represent, it will be hard to walk and operate in unity. Use wise discernment when building your team and ponder carefully who will make the best fit!

Finding Everything You Need
King David went to great lengths to prepare for the building of the house of the Lord. The directions he gave to his son Solomon provide an interesting insight into the topic....

"'As for you, my son Solomon, know the God of your father, and serve Him with a loyal heart and with a willing mind; for the Lord searches all hearts and understands all the intent of the thoughts. If you seek Him, He will be found by you; but if you forsake Him, He will cast you off forever. Consider now, for the Lord has chosen you to build a house for the sanctuary; be strong, and do it.' "

"Then David gave his son Solomon the plans for the vestibule, its houses, its treasuries, its upper chambers, its inner chambers, and the place of the mercy seat; and the plans for all that he had by the Spirit, of the courts of the house of the Lord..."

"'All this,' said David, 'the Lord made me understand in writing, by His hand upon me, all the works of these plans.' And David said to his son Solomon, 'Be strong and of good courage, and do it; do not fear nor be dismayed, for the Lord God, my God, will be with you. He will not leave you nor forsake you, until you have finished all the work for the service of the house of the Lord. Here are the divisions of the priests and the Levites for all the service of the house of God; and every willing craftsman will be with you for all manner of workmanship, for every kind of service; also the leaders and all the people will be completely at your command.' " -1 Chronicles 28:9-12 and 19-21

Comparatively, the faith-based business owner must likewise know the Lord, as well as serve and lead his company with a loyal heart and a willing mind. For there is nothing hidden before the Lord that He doesn't already know about or see (Hebrews 4:12-13). It is a great privilege to be chosen by the Lord to build a house (or in this case a business) in which the Lord shall be glorified! Like the king said, you must stop and consider such a thing.

Everything that Solomon needed, his father provided. Every plan, every detail, every measurement, every craftsman, every leader and every material necessary was set before him. Our heavenly Father has done the same for you. Everything that you need to glorify Him in a successful business, He has already placed before you. Use the building material found in His Word to guide you, for there is no thing too small or too great that the Lord cannot do for those whom He calls His own. Just as King David told his son, "If you seek Him, He will be found by you," the same applies to you. However, "If we forsake Him, He will cast us off forever." If that doesn't put the fear of the Lord in you, then we're not sure what will!

Notice how He says, "I will not leave you until you have finished all the work for the service of the house of the Lord." Friend, this is a lifelong commitment. You can be confident that what He has begun in you, He will complete in you (Philippians 1:6). But, you may not ultimately see that completion until you see Him face to face on the other side of eternity. The point... just keep building your temple: your personal body and the body of your business! (1 Corinthians 6:19) Whether the construction is ever 100% complete on earth is not the point, it's the construction process that matters most. How you build your business here and now is about the journey as well as the destination.

"Here are the priests, Levites, craftsman, leaders and all the people..." These were the essence of the building materials needed for the project. Wood, stone, silver and gold certainly weren't going to build themselves. King David went on to tell the assembly, "My son Solomon, whom alone God has chosen, is young and inexperienced; and the work is great, because the temple is not for man but for the Lord God." (1 Chronicles 29:1)

Your Father Knows What You Need
Solomon's father knew he would need strong men around him; not just as a labor force, but also as a support force for the vision that was set before him. Your Father knows the same regarding you; you need strong individuals around you that will support the call on your life and the vision for your company. Could you build it yourself? Maybe. But keep in mind, one may chase a thousand, but two can put ten thousand to flight. "For two are better than one, because they have a great reward for their labor. For if they fall, one will lift up his companion. But woe to him who is alone when he falls, for he has no one to help him up." (Ecclesiastes 4:9-10)

Letting Go Of What You Don't Need
If you believe the Scriptures provide you with everything you need in life and in your business, than you'd better believe they equally provide you with everything you don't need as well. It's easy to go to God asking for

things that we need or perhaps want. But, what about asking Him to remove the things we don't need?

In God's design less is usually more. Yes, it's contrary to man's traditional way of thinking, but remember, "God's ways are not our ways, nor are His thoughts our thoughts." (Isaiah 55:8-9). More employees, more payroll, more upkeep, more personalities, more spirits, more worries - more is not necessarily better. This doesn't mean don't grow or bring on additional staff, but simply look for opportunities to do more with less.

When it comes to building your team, we've discussed exposing the gifts, identifying the gifts, and placing the gifts. Now then, there is one thing to keep watch for despite the gifts of those who are around you. Understand that the gifts and calling of God are irrevocable (Romans 11:29). This means you may have a team member operating with an exceptional degree of success for your company when all the while they are in the backslidden state of a downward spiral going nowhere fast! It may not be grounds for dismissal at first, but keep watch that you or your employees don't get caught up in their counsel, lest you or the others get drawn back to some old familiar strongholds. Taking a walk, standing in their presence, or sitting at their dinner table is not what you need to keep you on track (Psalm 1:1-2). Play it safe, seek godly counsel, and keep the camp clean. No one is indispensable and this includes you.

"Blessed is the man who walks not in the counsel of the ungodly, nor stands in the path of sinners, nor sits in the seat of the scornful; but his delight is in the law of the Lord, and in His law he meditates day and night." - Psalm 1:1-2

CHAPTER TWENTY-THREE:
Identifying The Enemy

Spiritual Trouble Shooting

As we begin to conclude, there is one last subject of vital importance, which we must cover. Much has been covered throughout the David's 400 curriculum about managing yourself, your staff, and your business based on Biblical principles. As an entrepreneur, when you run your business according to God's will and God's ways, and are making a dent against the kingdom of darkness, know that there will be a variety of principalities and powers that will try to take you out or off course. Identifying what and who these spirits are is a vital priority for the faith-based company. Be prepared to find them inside your camp (you or your staff) as well as outside your borders (your clients or your competition).

You might consider this process as spiritual troubleshooting, godly warnings, enemy identification, or more simply put, spiritual discernment. Whatever the title, one thing is for sure; the idle mind cannot effectively function in this gift. Of course, anything and everything is possible, but having the gift and functioning in it are two different things. Understand, you may not have the supernatural gift of discerning spirits, but you'd better believe that God's Word is well able to reveal many things to those whose eyes are open to receive.

In these next few pages we'll expose some of the most stubborn, presumptuous, proudest, sneakiest, and dirtiest spirits revealed from the Scriptures.

Spiritual Discernment

The Holy Spirit can speak to you not only through the Scriptures themselves, but also through dreams, visions, and prophetic words. However, much of what is revealed by the Spirit comes through your capacity to perceive things correctly. The problem then lies in your ability (or inability) to purge yourself of your judgmental thoughts and reactions.

Spiritual discernment is the grace to see into the unseen, despite what you may think or feel. It is not a faculty of your own mind, but a gift of the Spirit to perceive what is in the Spirit. Discernment is when your spirit is telling you something your mind is not. To perceive, you must make yourself blind to what and how things appear.

Be reminded there is an adversary trying to deceive even God's elect if he can. To the church in Corinth, the apostle Paul put it this way, "For Satan himself transforms himself into an angel of light. Therefore it is no great thing if his ministers also transform themselves into ministers of righteousness, whose end will be according to their works." (2 Corinthians 11:14-15)

If you judge on the outward appearance only, you are likely to be fooled! True spiritual discernment cannot judge a book by its cover. On the contrary, you must get in The Book to uncover the true nature of what the Spirit is saying to you.

Spiritual discernment requires a heart of forgiveness. If you do not walk in genuine forgiveness, you will walk in much deception. You will presume you have discernment when, in truth, you are seeing through the veil of a critical spirit. Without true forgiveness, what you presume to discern in others is likely to be a reflection of yourself. For this reason, Christ said you must remove the log out of our own eye before you can pick the speck out of your brother's eye (Matthew 7:1-5). The judgmental, carnal mind will always see the image of itself in others, though never admitting it of course.

The bottom-line, if you want to see clearly, first make sure your own sightline of forgiveness and repentance is clear before God. Setting aside the natural instinct to condemn and judge others prematurely will open a door for the true gift of discernment to operate in you.

True discernment comes when your heart is still before the Lord. In order to hear from God, you must know that He is God. Hearing Him requires stillness, without strife, envy, fear, or ungodly suspicions. It is listening to the voice of the Holy Spirit as it aligns with God's Holy Word. This type of stillness is different from that of idleness. An idle person may sit still, but that doesn't mean his heart or mind is prepared to hear from God. On the contrary, the Word says that the idle mind is the devil's playground, not God's fertile ground. With that said, "Be still and know that He is God." (Psalm 46:10).

Godly discernment begins when godly motives are rooted in a committed love for the church and for one another. Love does not judge but corrects. It is the kind of love the Lord admonishes you with when you get sidetracked or go astray in your own mind. You are called to correct with love, not judge with condemnation. On the flip side, false discernment is always slow to hear, quick to speak, and quick to anger (James 1:19-20).

Discerning The Enemy
When you become sensitive to the Spirit, you become sensitive to the things in the spiritual realm. What happens when the spirit you discern is not your friend? The Bible draws a distinct line between angelic spirits and evil spirits. If you want to know whom you're fighting, you must be able to identify the nature of the spirit you are up against.

The Scriptures say that when Satan fell from heaven, he took one-third of the angels with him. That means there are numerous unclean spirits out there waiting to take you off course. This is not to scare you, but to make you aware of the things going on around you in the spiritual realm. Even with all these unclean spirits waiting to be discerned, it is important that you do not let that change your ultimate focus. The focus is to build your business on Biblical principles, not focus on every demon that comes within five feet of you or your establishment.

The work of the devil is to take your eyes off of Jesus and onto the distractions of this world, whether they are in the natural realm or spiritual realm. Satan's first weapon of attack always involves distraction. Redirecting your focus and turning your attention back to Jesus is what ultimately wins the battle at the end of the day. Remember the battle has already been won! Christ defeated Satan on the cross at Gethsemane, not by directly or verbally confronting the devil in that mere moment, but by fulfilling the destiny and call on His life! Friend, you have the victory in Christ when you walk according to the call that is on your life.

About Those Unclean Spirits
In the spirit realm, the name of something always corresponds to its nature. Take for example the names of God; each one uniquely describes His nature and His onama character. He is Jehovah-Jireh, our provider;

Jehovah-Rophe, our healer; Jehovah-Shalom, our peace; and Jehovah-Tsidkenu, our righteousness, just to name a few.

The same precept holds true for the enemies of God. Their very names will reveal what their nature and purpose are. Therefore, when you identify the enemy by name, you now have the advantage of knowing his tactic. Realize, his tactics are generally aimed at your weaknesses. In the following pages we intend to uncover a few of these sneaky, deceiving, unclean spirits, and exploit them according to what the Word of God says about their names and their nature.

Reveal The Name... Reveal The Nature!

So how do you discern when there is an unclean spirit within your midst? The Scriptures say, "You will know them by their fruits. Do men gather grapes from thorn bushes or figs from thistles? Even so, every good tree bears good fruit, but a bad tree bears bad fruit. A good tree cannot bear bad fruit, nor can a bad tree bear good fruit." (Matthew 7:16-18). If they say to you, "Look at what a beautiful apple tree I am," but the only thing you see growing from their branches is lemons... it's apparent you have a deceiver on your hands!

"LISTEN" ....To What They Say!
"WATCH" ....What They Do!
"THEN" ....You Will Know Who They Are!

Before going any further, it's important to keep this curriculum and its teachings in perspective. Is it always referring to someone else or have you examined yourself first to see if it is you that is being revealed? God will allow certain situations in your life to test your faith, to see what will manifest. Will you be able to perceive and recognize it when it comes? This is no time for idleness! The body of Christ, as well as the faith-based business owner, must do more than just recognize the apostate spirit; it must be called out or it will suck you in.

Recognize who you are breaking bread with and why. Is it to obtain a free meal with any and every demonic spirit that offers to pay, or is it for true fellowship and thanksgiving? Christ didn't beg Judas to stay, but told him,

"Go, do what you gotta do..." The pressure is on and this is no time to send Judas a sympathy card.

Traitors In The Camp: The Spirit Of Disloyalty

Wrong people in your life can create wrong seasons in your life. It is the enemy's number one focus breaker (distractions). Whoever has your ear has your future, and giving heed to wrong voices will ultimately lead to disloyalty. Are you aware of what or whom your staff members are listening to? Who has their ear? It is the choice to become disloyal that allows the spirit of rebellion to enter in.

The spirit of disloyalty becomes more susceptible to manifestation when the atmosphere lacks obvious successes or advances. People don't listen to negative voices when their ship is making headway. Apparent success, whether real or perceived, tends to keep the spirit of disloyalty at bay. However, once your agenda does not match their agenda, their true faces will begin to immerse. As stated previously, their faces have a name. In the Scriptures we see them as Lucifer, Judas, Absalom, and Jezebel to name a few.

Lucifer: This is the spirit and personality that cannot see his own weaknesses and flaws. Usually he is given extremely talented gifts (most often in the arts department). His creative side causes him to feel he is more important or has more seniority. When he falls, he'll take one third of the crowd with him.

Judas: This is the spirit that wants to succeed according to his way instead of God's way. He will support you as long as you do things his way. Once you offend him or refuse him, he will betray you and leave. Give him a rope and he'll hang himself every time.

Absalom: This is the ungrateful spirit that gets offended easily. He becomes like a garbage disposal for the grief of others; always willing to sit at the gate and listen to their complaints. He is unable to sit under submission and his major ambition is to steal the hearts of the people, taking them along with him in his rebellion. His rebellion is the byproduct of a spirit, which refuses to be corrected (he feels he is above it). He will sit in your enemy's presence and discuss you. His seduction is subtle; he will get to know you and your weaknesses so he can expose them at his opportune time. Others get emotionally attached to him because he appears lovable, nice, good looking, and popular. His motive is not about fellowship, but rather to influence and manipulate others to his agenda for his greater benefit.

Jezebel: This is the stubborn and ugly spirit of control and manipulation. It is more predominately found on a deceived woman, but it can equally overpower the manipulating men as well. She will woo you into making a decision that you think is your own, but in reality you have been manipulated and seduced into that decision. She will make you feel like you are in control, while behind the scenes she is doing all the controlling. She loves to talk to you about all the things that are wrong. Most of all, she will never leave until you stand up and confront her!

The name Jezebel means "unchaste, without cohabitation" or "Baal exalts." To be unchaste refers to being lewd, impure, defiled, and un-husbanded. Jezebel's name not only shows her character, it also foretells her way of life. She was infamous for her persistent idolatry and cruel persecution of the prophets. She was no doubt the queen of manipulation!

The spirit of Jezebel seeks control through words of manipulation and a body language of seduction (1 Kings 21:7-16, 2 Kings 9:30-31). Her desire is to rule and run headship for selfish gains. This spirit does not want to sit on the throne; it just wants to control the throne. There are definite places this spirit likes to dwell and certain characteristics it will feed on...

Jezebel's Breeding Ground
(1) Those who lack joy; constant complainers, negative about everything and everybody. (2) Those who are unteachable and resist change, preferring things just the way they are; don't rock their boat. (3) Those who have hidden agendas; not submitted to anyone else's agenda, prefer self-worship (aka: Baal worship). (4) Those who thrive in giving free reign to their carnal nature; gluttony, fornication, drunkenness, lewdness. (5) Those who are willing to give false testimony to further their own agenda; fabricators and exaggerators. (6) Those who surround themselves with fear, chaos, insecurity, frustration and confusion. (7) Those who dwell in destruction, despair and broken relationships; cesspool magnets. (8) Those who will fall for anything, yet stand for nothing.

Is there a breeding ground for this spirit in your business? Unless you are consistently diligent to keep things in check, this spirit will always look for ways to sneak in (usually in staff members in authoritative positions). You cannot be idle when it comes to the spirit of Jezebel! When you see the signs beginning to manifest, for your sake, do not tolerate it! This spirit hates confrontation. It may make you want to run and hide in a cave like Elijah rather than confront it. However, avoidance is not your answer! God said this spirit must be utterly and completely annihilated! So get your anointing oil out, pick up the sword of Jehu, and start the cutting process (figuratively speaking of course). If you don't, she will fervently attempt to take you and your whole company out!

Jezebel's Companion: The Spirit Of Control

The spirit of control works hard to manipulate other people, events, or circumstances to make things go her way. She is always trying to figure out how to spin, engineer, or manipulate situations to her advantage. When things don't go her way, she gets angry and upset. She believes everything might fall apart if it's not in her control; nothing will be done right without her direction or insight. Her way is the only right and proper way because it is what is in her best interest. This spirit overwhelms faith, squeezes out individual freedom, and grieves the Holy Spirit. Is this spirit starting to sound a little familiar? You know what to do, confront it and correct it. Remember, you cannot correct what you are not willing to confront!

The Spirit Of Pride & Presumption

The spirit of pride and presumption can be found in a number of characters throughout the Scriptures. King Uzziah was lifted up with pride when he presumed to enter the temple of the Lord to burn incense. In King Hezekiah's pride, he presumed to show off all his treasures to the enemy, only to have it stolen away. David's pride caused him to presume on the Lord when he numbered the children of Israel. Rehoboam's pride caused the kingdom to be split in two. The pride and presumption of Korah's rebellion caused the ground to literally swallow up him and his whole household. The list goes on and on, but none takes the cake more than the pride and presumption of King Saul.

The Spirit Of King Saul

You could consider King Saul the poster child for pride and presumption. His name means "desired" and that is exactly what he was, the people's choice (but not necessarily God's choice). The Scriptures say Saul was head and shoulders above the rest, and Saul certainly knew it. His pride and his presumption are the root of what led to his downfall.

You must first understand that Saul was anointed as a king, not as a priest. This means he was ordained for a specific post. If you should decide to operate outside the post God has anointed you for, then like Saul, you can expect grave consequences for that presumption. Saul's presumption manifested when he stepped out of his kingship role to offer a burnt sacrifice to the Lord. The problem was not only did he presume to act the part of the priest, but also he directly disobeyed the instructions given to him by the prophet Samuel.

"So Samuel said: 'Has the Lord as great delight in burnt offerings and sacrifices, as in obeying the voice of the Lord? Behold, to obey is better than sacrifice, and to heed than the fat of rams. For rebellion is as the sin of witchcraft, and stubbornness is as iniquity and idolatry. Because you have rejected the word of the Lord, He also has rejected you from being king.' " -1 Samuel 15:22-23

Many were caught in presumption before King Saul and many more were caught after him; for there is no temptation or sin that is uncommon to man (1 Corinthians 10:13). God is more concerned with your response to your presumption than the presumption itself.

When King David was caught in presumption, his response was humble acknowledgment and genuine repentance. King Saul, on the other hand, had a response of manly sorrow and emotional embarrassment.

It was Saul's response to his presumption that led to his rejection by God. If God is the same yesterday, today and forever, then He still delights in obedience more than sacrifice. The Lord is not looking for the sacrifice of your good works. He is looking for your obedience, even in the seemingly small things. The Word says that those who are diligent over little shall rule over much. Saul's inability to obey in the small things resulted in his rejection to rule over the large things, namely the Kingdom of Israel. This rejection was just the start of the downward spiral he was headed for.

Identifying The Spirit Of Saul
This spirit is all about pride and performance. It will go to the extent of setting up a monument for itself (1 Samuel 15:12), while declaring, "Look how great I am. Check out my amazing accomplishments." It will seek fake honor and flesh honor, but not the Father's honor. This spirit bears the fruit of jealousy, greed, paranoia, chaos, confusion, insanity, bitterness, revenge, and rebellion, just to name a few.

Saul's Specialty: Throwing Spears!
Watch out when this spirit becomes jealous. That is when his true nature begins to shine. It drives him crazy when others receive more attention than he does. Beware, for he has a few spears in his arsenal of madness waiting to throw your way. Correcting this spirit is difficult, for he does not like to be proven wrong, especially in front of others! He will do whatever it takes to keep his "head and shoulders above the rest" sort of prestige. On the flip side, if you need a star performer in a skit, he's definitely your man!

Spiritual Goats
Spiritual goats are full of pride and presumption as well as many other ungodly characteristics. They are a mix of Lucifer, Judas, Absalom, Jezebel, and Saul all put together. God makes a clear distinction between these goats and the rest of His flock.

"All the nations will be gathered before Him, and He will separate them one from another, as a shepherd divides his sheep from the goats. And He will set the sheep on His right hand, but the goats on the left." -Matthew 25:32-33

What is it about goats that cause God to despise them so much? Goats are stubborn, devious, impulsive, unpredictable, and very temperamental. If they are not climbing trees or butting heads with one another, they are eating everything and anything in sight. Goats are never content with what they have. They are experts in opening gates and squeezing through small gaps because they hate to be confined. They will work tirelessly to spring themselves from any situation they deem inhibiting. They are self-willed and refuse to obey authority without threats or demands. Consequently, goats are not good followers! They would rather lead or go off on their own. When goats are mixed with the sheepfold, they become very territorial. They will herd and dominate the sheep, creating stress and excitement in the flock. Sound like anyone you know?

Spiritual goats will confess to know the Holy Spirit, but by their own words and deeds deny Him. Without the hand of God on their lives, they pretend pseudo outward obedience to protect their own flesh and hidden motives. Goats are nothing more than stumbling blocks and unity breakers. Their own stubborn pride keeps them from repentance for fear of looking bad in front of the other goats or being exposed before the sheep. From goat's milk to sheep's wool, God will eventually separate the two. As a faith-based company, you would do well to do the same. Just make sure it is in God's timing and with His discernment.

Authority Over Disloyalty

Now that you have a better understanding of what to look for in some of these troubling spirits, it is time to take action. Remember, you cannot correct what you are not willing to confront and you cannot complain about that which you tolerate. Identify the unclean spirits around you and resolve to take action according to the Word of God. Be sensitive to the Holy Spirit and His promptings. When you see these characteristics rise up in yourself, be humble enough to acknowledge it, and genuine enough to repent from it.

Watch out for impostors. They may come in looking like servants, but given time, their true nature will manifest. Avoid promoting people until their character is proven. Mark those who cause division and avoid them all together. They are a detriment to any business. Leave vengeance to the Lord. The disloyalty of the prideful will be brought down on their own heads.

The Stages Of Disloyalty That You Need To Keep A look Out For

Stage 1: Independence
They begin to do what they want when they want. They interpret your instructions rather than follow them. Their tardiness is a form of silent rebellion.

Stage 2: Offended
They become easily offended by the smallest and most insignificant things. They usually end up sharing these offenses with those who are around them.

Stage 3: Uninvolved
They slowly begin to draw back. They become full of excuses. They don't show up for company meetings or functions. They skip out on anything that's considered voluntary.

Stage 4: Critical
They start to question your decisions and cause you to doubt yourself. They will seek to find another in your organization that has become disgruntled with your leadership.

Stage 5: Political

They will hide their own moral issues behind a mask of being overly holy; all the while accusing you of everything they themselves do in the dark. They are looking for someone to come into agreement with their rebellion. Their agenda is all about their own political power.

Operating a faith-based company is not easy. It takes courage! May God give you such courage and the endurance to see it through. You have the unique ability to change the way Christianity is viewed in the business arena. Will you be a voice for Him in your faith-based company? You can not do it sitting idle, so get out there and start living what you believe in the business arena!

It is our ambition that this David's 400 Curriculum has clearly and effectively taught God's Biblical revelations in a way that will influence how you run your business. When God's Word goes forth, He promises that it will not return void or empty, but it will accomplish what He pleases, and it will prosper in the thing for which He sent it. We agree, in prayer, that it is His good pleasure to pour out blessings on His entrepreneurs who obediently and willingly operate their endeavors in faith and by faith. To God be all the glory!

Resource Material

"Every good gift and every perfect gift is from above, and comes down from the Father of lights, with whom there is no variation or shadow of turning." -James 1:17

"Both riches and honor come from You, and You reign over all. In Your hand is power and might; In Your hand it is to make great and to give strength to all. Now therefore, our God, we thank You and praise Your glorious name. But who am I, and who are my people, that we should be able to offer so willingly as this? For all things come from You, and of Your own we have given You." -1 Chronicles 29:12-14

We humbly acknowledge that there is nothing we have that we did not receive. The following is a list of resources that inspired various content within this book.

God's Holy Word, NKJV, New Sprit Filled Life Bible and the Word Wealth and Kingdom Dynamics contained within It.

Joshua Commentary by James Montgomery Boice

Nehemiah Commentary by James Montgomery Boice

Thru The Bible by James Vernon McGee

Overcoming The Seduction Of Disloyalty by Dr. Jerry Grillo, Jr.

Strong's Exhaustive Concordance Of The Bible

Blueletterbible.org

Dictionary.com

Countless teachings, sermons, and personal discipleship by Bishop M.L.Moody, Redeemed International Church

God's precious Holy Spirit, which leads us into all truth!